PRAISE FOR *LEAD WITH HEART*

"*Lead with Heart* offers poignant, heartfelt lessons about being an authentic leader, and doing it with compassion, trust, commitment, care, and warmth. It is a brilliant clarion call—and a must-read!"
—Molly Biwer, senior vice president of public affairs and communications at Hallmark

"Tom graciously and humbly describes his journey from a mind-set of valuing results over relationships to one that recognizes that relationships always proceed results. It's a handbook for any leader seeking sustained organizational excellence over short-term achievements by capturing people's hearts rather than commanding their hands. I heartily (pun intended!) endorse it!"
—Dave Ridley, former chief marketing officer at Southwest Airlines

"In this inspiring book, Tom brings to life—through compelling personal stories and powerful leadership lessons—'When you focus on people, the profits will follow.' He realized that his transformation as a leader was occurring when he was able to walk into a room and say, 'Hey, look at you!' instead of 'Hey, look at me.' This book is a must-read for all leaders . . . and for those who strive to find the leader within themselves."
—Captain D. Michael Abrashoff, former commander USS *Benfold*, and *New York Times* and *Wall Street Journal* business bestselling author of *It's Your Ship*

"*Lead with Heart* is a fantastic, crystal clear look into how Tom built the foundation of his highly successful leadership style by focusing on his character and inherent values. There is no doubt this book will enlighten any leader and help them transform their business through personal connection. I had a behind-the-scenes look at the positive impact his approach had professionally with his team at Avis, and how family extended well beyond the Gartland name. I am personally fortunate that leading with heart has no boundaries—and because of that, our friendship to this day is genuine and real.

—Steve Stricker, pro golfer and US Captain
for the 2017 Presidents Cup

"*Lead with Heart* captures the phenomenal power of personal authenticity to effect change on those with whom you interact. But even more importantly, it gives you the tools to recognize and apply these leadership principles in your own life. You can use them to chart a new course starting now!"

—Chris Soder, former CEO and president
of Priceline.com, Inc.

"Tom knows that strategy without culture does not exist and culture without committed and engaged team members is meaningless. *Lead with Heart* is an inspiring reminder to each of us of what it takes to move an organization—and yourself—to accomplish greater things in work and in life."

—Adam Johnson, chairman and CEO of NetJets

"*Lead with Heart* shines a bright light on what it really means to be a highly effective leader. In sharing deeply personal experiences, and placing relationships at the center of his life, Tom sets a powerful example for leaders. If you want to win in life or business you must first win the hearts of your teammates.

—Paul Grunau, chief learning officer at APi Group

LEAD WITH HEART

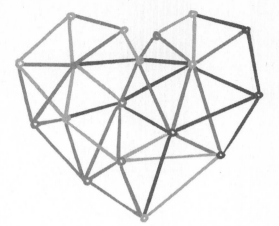

LEAD WITH HEART

TRANSFORM YOUR BUSINESS THROUGH PERSONAL CONNECTION

TOM GARTLAND

WITH PATRICK SWEENEY

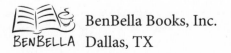

BenBella Books, Inc.
Dallas, TX

BenBella

BenBella Books, Inc.
10440 N. Central Expressway, Suite 800
Dallas, TX 75231
www.benbellabooks.com
Send feedback to feedback@benbellabooks.com

Printed in the United States of America
10 9 8 7 6 5 4 3 2 1

Library of Congress Cataloging-in-Publication Data
Names: Gartland, Tom, author. | Sweeney, Patrick, 1952- author.
Title: Lead with heart : transform your business through personal connection
   / Tom Gartland, with Patrick Sweeney.
Description: Dallas, TX : BenBella Books, Inc., [2018] | Includes
   bibliographical references and index.
Identifiers: LCCN 2017052641 (print) | LCCN 2017054659 (ebook) | ISBN
   9781946885258 (electronic) | ISBN 9781946885005 (trade cloth : alk. paper)
Subjects: LCSH: Personnel management. | Leadership. | Corporate culture.
Classification: LCC HF5549 (ebook) | LCC HF5549 .G3195 2018 (print) | DDC
   658.4/092—dc23
LC record available at https://lccn.loc.gov/2017052641

Editing by Leah Wilson and Debbie Harmsen
Copyediting by James Fraleigh
Proofreading by Lisa Story and Chris Gage
Text design and composition by Aaron Edmiston
Cover design and illustration by Faceout Studio, Spencer Fuller
Jacket design by Sarah Avinger
Printed by Lake Book Manufacturing

Distributed to the trade by Two Rivers Distribution, an Ingram brand
www.tworiversdistribution.com

Special discounts for bulk sales (minimum of 25 copies) are available.
Please contact Aida Herrera at aida@benbellabooks.com.

With Love
And All My Heart
To
Barb
Sara, David, Tomás
Kevin, Whitney, Avery, Jackson
Lizzie, Joe, Vincent
Henry, Abbi
Barbell Mel

CONTENTS

Foreword   xiii

Introduction   xvii

CHAPTER 1

Learning to Lead with Heart   1

CHAPTER 2

Knowing the Sound of Your Own Heart   15

CHAPTER 3

Opening Yourself Up—to Yourself and to Others   33

CHAPTER 4

Building an Engaged, Trusting Culture   51

CHAPTER 5

Sometimes It Takes Being Friggin' Crazy   67

CHAPTER 6

Recognizing the Potential in People   87

CHAPTER 7

Delivering Tough News with Your Heart   119

CHAPTER 8

Creating a Purpose and Strategy
That Connects with Your Team   145

CHAPTER 9

Connecting with the Hearts of Your Customers   165

CHAPTER 10

Seeing New Possibilities with Your Coach   185

Conclusion   205
My Scorecard Update   211
A Special Lifelong Connection   215
Acknowledgments   219
About the Authors   221

FOREWORD

I've had the pleasure of knowing Tom Gartland since 2012, when Avis first became a marketing partner of the PGA Tour. Avis continues to be a valued sponsor for the Tour, and we have Tom largely to thank for making it happen.

What was apparent about Tom from the outset was that when he has a vested interest in a business relationship, he's all in. The commitment of Tom and his team was absolute, and it helped set the foundation for what has proven to be a lasting, mutually rewarding association. In looking back, our dealings also provided insight into the corporate culture that Tom instilled at Avis, which in turn was reflective of the leadership philosophy he describes in this book.

I believe our organizations have worked well together in large part because of commonality in priorities and the way we respect and work with our employees and partners. Although the PGA Tour grew from a small operation to a multi-faceted, global organization, my predecessor, Deane Beman, and I strived to maintain a family culture that emphasized a strong connection with our employees, cele-bration of successes, and giving back to others.

What Tom was able to do at Avis, remarkably, was instill that same close-knit, family philosophy throughout a corporation with several thousand locations and twenty thousand employees. I knew of his reputation as an out-standing executive. But it's the story of how he got there, the self-enlightenment that ultimately became the driving force behind his leadership at Avis, that is truly fascinating.

While there are countless books on the topic of leader-ship, it's rare that one comes along that provides such unique perspective. The approach he purposely adopted when he came to Avis was bold and unconventional, for sure. As the title implies, *Lead with Heart* abandons the mentality that leaders shouldn't stray beyond their confidants within the organization and get too close to others. Instead, he believed that building strong relationships, outwardly demonstrating compassion and care, would permeate the entire organiza-tion and create a thriving, productive workplace.

I admire Tom for taking such a brave, unconventional approach to "humanize" his leadership, and *Lead with Heart* is an entertaining and informative read to better understand the reaction of his team members, from the doubts to full acceptance of his authenticity to adapting the same philos-ophy themselves.

I know you'll enjoy this remarkable journey and gain valuable insight from Tom's bold departure from the norm in corporate leadership.

—TIM FINCHEM, Former PGA Tour Commissioner

INTRODUCTION

I was a leader for two decades before I learned that *leading with my heart* was the key to unlocking my true leadership potential. It has helped me create a thriving, engaged culture; advance a purpose and strategy that inspires top performance; and live an integrated, whole life, where my personal values are in alignment with work realities and where life at work and life at home are not in two separate boxes. What transformed me as a leader was learning how to connect my head with my heart. Once I made that connection, everything changed. I was able to connect deeply with my heart and the hearts of others. I even became comfortable with a word that you seldom hear in a business setting: *love*.

The ancient Greek philosophers defined one of the highest forms of love as the deep, comradely relationships that develop when you see yourself in others; are there for each other; share your beliefs, your thoughts, and your emotions; and feel the loyalty created when you strive to succeed together for a noble cause in which you mutually believe.

This is the kind of love I am talking about. It's the kind of love that is behind leading with heart. It's the kind of love that allows us leaders to be vulnerable and courageous enough to truly open ourselves up, allowing those around us to see who we really are. And it was with this kind of love that I helped to transform the culture of a Fortune 500 company into an engaged, collaborative, top-performing organization that experienced unprecedented growth.

OPEN-HEART SURGERY?

I firmly believe that the time has come for us to get comfortable with how our hearts can transform our lives—personally and professionally—because while the ancient Greek concept of love is timeless, learning how to lead with our hearts turns out to be brand new for each of us. It becomes a personal journey. Very personal. It was for me. And, I assure you, it will be for you, as well.

For many of us as leaders, I am keenly aware that opening our hearts and being vulnerable would be the emotional equivalent to open-heart surgery. But, I assure you, opening your heart is worth it—for you, and for those around you.

My goal is to show you how to open up to your true leadership potential. I am not promising you that leading with heart will be easy. But I can promise you that learning to lead with heart will make you much more connected, more open, and more honest with yourself—and, as a result, more authentic to those around you.

My goal is to help you discover those connections—within yourself, and with others—so that you can become a leader worth following.

WHAT TO EXPECT IN THIS BOOK

In this book, I will share personal stories and insights to demonstrate to you what leading with heart looks like. You'll see the importance of connecting with your heart, opening up to others, being more trusting and collaborative, and deepening your connections. You'll also see the value in blending your personal life with your professional life.

My leadership journey is about the transformation that occurred when I, who was once a typically disconnected leader, learned to lead with my heart. My intent is to openly share with you how I came to purposely blur the lines between work and life, and, how, by leading with my heart, I was able to bring about improved relationships, work cultures, and bottom lines.

By opening my heart to those with whom I collaborate—and, just as important, being genuinely concerned with what is going on in *their* hearts—I have found the results can be astounding. I will share some of these remarkable transformations with you. In fact, you'll hear from many of the team members I worked with when I was a leader at Avis Budget Group, first as executive vice president of sales, marketing, and customer care and then as president, North America.

This is not your typical business book. I'm not offering a ten-step formula or case studies from myriad companies. I'm not packing these pages with quantitative proof that being kind, open, and honest with everyone, personally and professionally, will affect your bottom line (though I will share with you how it will do exactly that). I am writing this book to inspire you through my story of learning to lead with heart, and to share with you the valuable lessons I learned along the way. In this book I talk about opening up with people, and I am going to do just that with you as well.

My fervent hope in sharing my journey (including the lessons I learned and some very personal stories) is for you to be able to recognize how *you* can lead with your heart and become more of the leader you are meant to be—earlier and more easily than I did. My being completely personal, open, and vulnerable with you throughout the book is at the heart of my message—connect with your heart, so you can connect with the hearts of others.

By learning to lead with heart, you will come to see a world of new possibilities in yourself and in others. My desire is that, in the process, as your connections deepen, you will see your measures of success—including leading a more fulfilled life, your employees' engagement scores, and your organization's profits—exceed your expectations.

A PREVIEW OF WHAT'S TO COME

Chapter 1: Learning to Lead with Heart. I used to follow an unwritten rule of business that says leaders need to keep a safe distance between themselves and those they are leading. *Don't let your guard down or they might lose respect for you.* I was rising in the ranks as a leader, but leading that way was leaving me hollow. I have come to learn that when we as leaders follow that rule, we become disconnected from those we are leading, which inevitably lowers morale, erodes trust, diminishes engagement, squelches collaboration, and, ultimately, shrinks the bottom line. I wanted to lead in a way that aligned with my values. I call this new leadership approach leading with heart.

Chapter 2: Knowing the Sound of Your Own Heart. Leading with heart begins with understanding your driving story. What do you need to prove? To yourself? And to others? What stories do you believe helped to shape who you are? As I share with you what I learned about myself, particularly what was driving me, I will also challenge you to consider the depth and meaning of your leadership story. Do you know how to connect where you have been with where you are going? Are you comfortable sharing the personal stories and lessons you have learned on your leadership journey? Are your values driving where you are going? This is what I call "knowing the sound of your own heart."

Chapter 3: Opening Yourself Up—to Yourself and to Others. We then explore how to become more open and connected. For me, this transformation came when I assumed a new leadership position at Avis, moving with my wife to a new part of the country. I saw it as an ideal opportunity to reinvent myself and lead in a new way that would be much more fulfilling professionally and personally. This was also where I began to seamlessly blend the professional and personal aspects of my life and, in the process, become truer to myself and others.

Chapter 4: Building an Engaged, Trusting Culture. Trust is the measure of any relationship's strength. Many leaders, though, prefer to surround themselves with just a few "trusted" advisors, treating trust like a rare commodity. I was more interested in creating an engaged, trusting culture, where everyone felt like they were a vital part of our success. So, I knew that I needed to be the starting place for trust to flourish on a deeper level. But how could I make that happen?

Chapter 5: Sometimes It Takes Being Friggin' Crazy. As trust grew in our organization, we were coming through for our customers. But something was missing. There was not a feeling of "us," a shared sense of purpose. I knew that we needed to find a way to connect more deeply with each other. In this chapter, I share the idea I came up with that one of my colleagues said was "friggin' crazy." And I encourage you to come up with your own "friggin' crazy" ideas so that you can connect with the heart of your organization.

Chapter 6: Recognizing the Potential in People. As leaders, our goal is to see in others something that they might not even be aware of: their potential. Identifying potential and developing talent is, I believe, the most important contribution you can make to your organization. Yet when we as new leaders are seeking recognition and accomplishments ourselves, it can be hard for us to see that leading is not about us. It is about others. I will share with you how this transformation finally transpired for me. It kicked in when I was able to walk into a room saying, "Hey, look at you!" instead of thinking, "Hey, look at me." Learning how to make it about "you"—rather than about "me"—was a major breakthrough. It was like seeing the world in Technicolor for the first time. That shift in my perspective also enabled me to see those around me in a new light. Most importantly, I was able to see their real potential. In this chapter, we explore the importance of recognizing the qualities that distinguish your top performers, while also looking at your organization's high-potential individuals with a long-term view, connecting their aspirations with your organization's future.

Chapter 7: Delivering Tough News with Your Heart. While leading with heart can open leaders up to connecting with people on a much deeper level, many leaders default to keeping a safe distance between themselves and those around them because they do not want to find themselves in the awkward position of having a difficult conversation with someone who has become a friend. Of course, we don't want to hurt anyone else's feelings. In this chapter I share insights into how to deliver tough news from your heart, including difficult conversations I had with individuals that surprised and transformed them—personally and professionally. With honesty and trust as your foundation, you can have difficult conversations in a way that is caring and sincere, with the best interests of both the individual and your organization at heart.

Chapter 8: Creating a Purpose and Strategy That Connects with Your Team. While my emphasis is on people, I believe that succeeding in business starts with a compelling purpose and a clearly articulated strategy. This is where we, as leaders, connect our heads with our hearts. For others to follow you, they need to *believe* in three things: you, your organization's purpose, and your strategy for succeeding. Do they believe they can trust you? Do they believe what you are doing together is important? And do they believe in your master plan? When the answers to those three questions are clear and unconditional, then the right people will be drawn to your organization, enthused to be part of its journey and success, knowing they can play a vital role.

Chapter 9: Connecting with the Hearts of Your Customers. In this chapter, I share how the connections I have made with customers have led to some of my closest friendships. But such deep feelings need to come from the inside out. Before your customers feel valued, connected, and enthused about referring you to others, you must start with the heart of your organization. Your customers' experiences are a direct reflection of the internal culture you have created. When trusting, open, and compassionate relationships permeate your organization, they spread naturally to the outside—to your clients, business partners, and prospects. That is when you are ready to truly connect with your customers, opening yourself up to the possibility that your relationship can enhance your lives. Do not look for the sale, look for the connection. Engage. And be there *entirely*. That is how you stand out from the crowd. Then, as your relationship evolves, you will become partners. When you open yourself up to truly connecting with others, those connections can become as deep as they are wide. That is why I firmly believe that business is personal. *Very personal.*

Chapter 10: Seeing New Possibilities with Your Coach. To stay connected and to keep honing your leadership gifts, I firmly believe that every leader needs a coach. A coach can help you to candidly and objectively explore your concerns, doubts, blind spots, aspirations, and dreams—while helping you stay focused on what is most important for your organization and your personal growth. Particularly if you are going to lead with your heart, a coach can help you explore new options, while occasionally offering unvarnished advice that you need to hear. A coach's questions, such as—*How does this decision confirm your values?*—asked at just the right time, can shed new light on a situation you are grappling with and help you see new possibilities.

ASKING YOURSELF QUESTIONS

Throughout the book, including at the end of each chapter, I will ask you questions and also provide questions for you to ask yourself about how you can trust, open up, and connect more—with yourself and those around you. Like the questions in most of the important tests in our lives, these are not true-or-false or multiple-choice questions. The answers are yours, and yours alone. Just keep in mind that the questions we ask ourselves, and how deeply we answer them, help to shape who we become. With that in mind, I encourage you to dive deeply as you explore these questions. Then review your answers from time to time. And allow your answers to evolve—they will serve as road signs on your leadership journey.

LEAD WITH HEART

CHAPTER 1
LEARNING TO LEAD WITH HEART

Early in my career, like most leaders I have come to know, I kept a comfortable distance between myself and those I was leading. Those relationships, I felt, were *professional*. So, I kept them safely at arm's length, not close like my *personal* relationships. No one had explained to me that framing my world in such a way was an unwritten rule of leadership; I had learned this lesson through osmosis. Somehow, I just knew that it was important for me, as a leader, to keep my personal and professional lives safely separate. Sure, on occasions, I would let my guard down and get a little closer to some of my colleagues, but in the back of my mind, there was always a hesitation about getting too close.

Although there was no written rule, the not-so-subtle message I and other leaders definitely had received was that if we dared to blur our professional and personal relationships, we would lose an essential part of our ability to lead. Our underlying concern was that being more open about ourselves and more connected with others could be a slippery slope. We could lose our objectivity, and people might call our capacity to hold others accountable into question. We could end up playing "favorites," and those whom we favored would get an easy pass.

We also might appear vulnerable if we opened ourselves up, which would eliminate the mystery of leadership. If we let down our guard, others might see our soft spots and shortcomings. Worse yet, we might appear weak, fallible—perhaps even expendable.

This overriding concern was strong enough to keep most of us at a safe, professional distance from those we were leading. Why question it? There seemed to be little benefit, and much risk, to letting those we were leading see what was behind the curtain.

Added to this, I must admit that early in my career, I was consumed with becoming a leader. So, my focus was on my destiny—rather than on bringing those around me along for the journey. That, too, is a leadership lesson that took me quite a while to learn—or, rather, to unlearn.

DISTANCING OURSELVES CAUSES THOSE AROUND US TO BECOME DISENGAGED

Although the rule about leaders keeping their personal and professional lives separate is unwritten, it is pervasive and quietly destructive. My transformation as a leader began when I started to question it.

When we as leaders keep a safe, professional distance between ourselves and those we are leading, it destroys trust, collaboration, careers, and the very fabric of our organizations. I have come to believe that leaders who keep their personal and professional lives in separate boxes are at the heart of what is wrong with most organizations. I will even go so far as to say that such leaders are one of the primary reasons that more than four out of five people working in organizations are either not fully engaged or actively disengaged.

When those who follow us do not know what is inside of us, how can we possibly expect them to be genuinely engaged? (Think of how you feel when you are talking with someone whose thoughts, feelings, and attention seem to be elsewhere.) When our hearts are not open, we are not truly connected—to ourselves or to others. So, such disconnected leaders unwittingly send the clear message that we are not "all in." And those around us can sense our distance a mile away.

The result, not surprisingly, is that those within such organizations follow their leaders' behavior: they, too, hold themselves back. Why wouldn't they? Then such leaders wonder why everyone in their organizations is not more engaged. They may try to improve the organization's "engagement scores" by providing a new benefit or introducing what they believe is an innovative incentive program. Then, a few months later, they scratch their heads in dismay when the new program has no measurable impact on their employees' engagement scores.

Why in the world would we expect those we work with to give it their all if they do not experience us showing up completely? *True commitment only comes when there is a true connection.*

WHAT ABOUT WORK/LIFE BALANCE?

Separating our personal and professional lives has created a false dichotomy—a schism that damages how we conduct business and the results we intend to achieve. It is little wonder why we and our colleagues have such difficulty trying to balance our lives with our work. Part of it is because we see our personal and professional lives as completely separate expressions of our selves.

Actually, I believe the very phrase "work/life balance" highlights the problem that so many leaders have promulgated. Simply stated, it is this: we have created a gulf—in ourselves and thus in those who are trying to follow us—between *who we are* and *what we are doing.* To me, the concept of trying to balance our lives and our work conjures the image of someone cautiously trying to walk on a tightrope, precariously holding on to a pole, as they sway back and forth. It is the image of someone ready to fall over when the slightest gust of wind comes along, as it always does.

I have come to believe that true success does not come from separating who we are from what we are doing. True success comes from blending and prioritizing. That is why *true leadership starts with letting those we are leading see who we really are,* and with investing in and knowing who they are—personally and professionally. Successful leaders don't build walls between themselves and those they lead; they build bridges of understanding and support. They show that they want their employees to succeed; they make everyone feel like part of the family. When leaders do this, their employees are engaged, and their organizations climb to new heights. Conversely, our organizations suffer when too many people *love leading* but don't understand how to *lead with love.*

I want to emphasize that most of us, as leaders, do not intend to send the very negative, strong, and clear message that we are not completely committed to the success of our employees. Most of us do not even realize that we are holding back part of ourselves. Some of us may even be very approachable and willing to openly share our *thoughts.* But if we also send the clear message that our *feelings* are off limits, then we are far from open. And by holding our cards close to our vest, we unintentionally but inevitably create an environment that is lacking in trust—which, of course, is the bedrock of any strong relationship. Certainly, we do not do this on purpose. We are just following that old rule of leadership about keeping a safe distance between ourselves and others.

The truth is, you can achieve some levels of success without leading from your heart. I led that way for decades. You can even make your way up the leadership ladder following the old rule. In fact, not knowing about leading with my heart did not stop me from becoming the president of a billion-dollar company early in my career. But the way I was leading was leaving me hollow. I knew there had to be a better way.

QUESTIONING THE RULE, LEADING A NEW WAY

Learning to lead with heart was not an overnight discovery for me. In fact, it took the lion's share of my career for me to realize this important lesson. I believe it is the most valuable lesson I have learned as a leader.

It took becoming president of Avis Budget Group, North America, for me to finally allow myself to be me. That was when my real leadership ability started to evolve. To be me, I realized I could no longer keep my heart at a safe distance from those around me. To lead with my heart, I needed to break this unwritten rule about not getting too close to the people who were "reporting" to me.

Everything about the way I was leading started to change when I allowed myself to connect more deeply with my own feelings, to share what was inside of me, and to care passionately about the people with whom I was working shoulder to shoulder. I purposely began to care about, connect more deeply with, and (a word I use often) *love* the people with whom I had the privilege of working. Learning to lead with heart involved a process of becoming more comfortable with and confident in who I was becoming.

I came to understand that finding "the personal" in my relationships is the key to succeeding in business—as it is in life. There is absolutely no need for us, as leaders, to separate our personal lives from our professional lives. All that separation does is keep us disconnected—from ourselves and from those around us. Life and work are not separate parts of ourselves. We need to truly connect the *who* with the *what*. We need to connect *who* we are with *what* we are doing in order to succeed personally and professionally.

I wish I'd known about leading with heart earlier in my career. This lesson, however, was not even hinted at in any of the leadership training I underwent. In fact, this lesson runs counter to virtually everything I'd learned about being a leader.

Again, I am not saying that you cannot lead without connecting your head with your heart. Plenty of people do. What I am most interested in, though, is leading in a way that, while it may seem new, is full of the kind of love—including openness, collaboration, and trust—that the ancient Greeks defined a long time ago. I am drawn to lead in a way that inspires us to see ourselves in others, so that we are there for each other, with depth in our relationships that develops because we are striving to succeed together in a noble cause in which we believe—with all of our hearts.

That is what it means to lead with heart.

I have found that when we truly open up and care about the people we work with, we can transform organizations into sanctuaries where people feel a deep connection to one another, a profound sense of being part of an important mission, and extraordinary engagement in their work.

But how can we measure our success?

YOUR PERSONAL SCORECARD

Every successful person I have met has his or her own "scorecard"—that individual's personal and professional measure of success. *Your scorecard is your personal measure of what is important to you.* It is the way you keep track of how you're doing. Everyone needs to decide on their own the key categories for their scorecard, so yours generally will have several unique measurements. You can determine these by asking yourself questions such as: What is important to me? What do I love doing? What drives me? Am I being true to myself? Am I happy? Are my professional successes connected to my personal values?

While these may not seem like typical leadership questions, they are exactly the right place to start your scorecard and measure your success. You will need self-awareness and guts to answer such questions honestly. These types of questions are worth asking yourself regularly—on a personal *and* a professional level—particularly if you want to *lead with your heart.*

One of my key measures of success is the depth of my connections. Another one is related to how much time I spend with my family. You may have different key measures, which may evolve with you over time; my scorecard changed dramatically when I learned how to lead with my heart. What matters for now is that you are crystal clear about how your scorecard measures your own personal and professional success.

When I began to learn about leading with heart, I saw that the priorities in my scorecard needed to change. First and foremost, my work priorities and my personal values had to become more aligned.

How can you get clear about your own scorecard? You need to be true to yourself. As one of my first mentors, Jack Lachenmayer, reminded me, at the end of the day, when you look in the mirror, do you like what you see? Did you give it your all today? Are you living your values? That is what you need to measure.

Ultimately, it is up to you to create your own scorecard, then measure for yourself how you are doing.

WHEN WE FOCUS ON PEOPLE, THE PROFITS WILL FOLLOW

I mentioned how the depth of my connections is one of my key measures of success. The reason is because I firmly believe that deep connections will always open up new possibilities, both in business and in life. My philosophy and my experience have confirmed that *when we focus on people, the profits will follow*.

Not surprisingly, when people hear that phrase, I am often asked whether I can quantify the success of leading with my heart. So, let me quickly share some results. By the end of my first year of leading with heart at Avis Budget Group, North America, our employee engagement scores went up so high that the research scientist who did the survey said, "We have never seen results move like this in thirty years." And over the course of the next two years, those scores became "world class," improving by 14 percent during the three years I was that division's president. Our employees were engaged, connected, and coming through—for themselves, for one another, and for our customers.

And by giving it their all, our employees increased our revenue by 21 percent, while also improving our EBITDA by 31 percent during those three years. Also, as a significant part of Avis Budget Group, our North America team drove shareholder value as reflected in a rise in share price (NASDAQ: CAR) from $17.73 to $68.66. Our customers were feeling the warmth as well, as demonstrated by significantly improved J.D. Power scores.

Through the connections we were creating with one another and with our various business partners and customers, we were instilling trust, raising engagement levels, and having fun, while also defying gravity. This is how I know unequivocally that *when you focus on people, the profits will follow.*

ARE YOU READY TO LEAD WITH HEART?

I firmly believe that the time has come for us to get comfortable with how our hearts can transform our lives—personally

and professionally. Together, I contend, we can revolution-
ize how we lead by opening our hearts. Such leadership is
actually a better match for the global, collaborative, inter-
dependent, and interconnected world in which we all live.

Let me close this chapter with this thought: start to consider what could happen if you begin to open your heart to
those around you—and to listen to what is in their hearts.
Imagine the impact that could have on your company's culture, and how that effect could ripple. Envision yourself
leading in an organization where people are more open and
committed—believing in themselves, trusting each other,
feeling truly engaged, coming through—as together you
deliver memorable experiences for your clients and create
new possibilities for your company.

Just imagine.

It all starts with opening your heart.

SAY THE WORD "LOVE"

One very simple way to *lead with your heart* is to say the word "love" out loud in one of your next meetings. What do you love about what someone just said or did? Say it out loud.

I recognize that "love" is not a word that is often used in corporate settings. But when you start saying the word "love," surprising things will begin to happen. Simply by sharing this word that is so personally connected with your feelings, you will begin to change the depth of your conversations. Then a shift will occur. At first it may seem subtle. Then it will become significant as you begin to open yourself up to loving those around you, loving what you are accomplishing together, loving where you have been, loving where you are, and loving where you are going.

Opening your heart to this kind of love, I believe, can change the culture, purpose, and results of your organization.

My hope is that you open yourself up to such possibilities.

LEARNING TO LEAD WITH HEART: QUESTIONS FOR SELF-EVALUATION

The questions we ask ourselves, and how deeply we answer them, help to shape who we become. With that in mind, I encourage you to dive deeply as you explore these questions. Then review your answers from time to time. And allow your answers to evolve. Your answers will serve as road signs on your leadership journey.

1. How do you measure your success?
2. Have you created your own scorecard?
3. What is important to you?
4. What do you love doing?
5. Are you being true to yourself?
6. Did you give it your all today?
7. Are you living your values?
8. Do you update your scorecard and allow it to change over time?

CHAPTER 2

KNOWING THE SOUND OF YOUR OWN HEART

Leading with heart starts with *listening to your heart*. Do you know what that beating sound is trying to tell you? Are you aware of what really drives you? Do you know what you need to prove? To yourself? To others?

Everyone has something that drives him or her. I call this their *driving story*. It is at the heart of who they are. Do you know what your story is? It is important that you know the depth and meaning of your driving story. What is the story deep inside of you that illuminates you, making you known, understood, and worth following? Your story expresses who you are, where you are from, where you are going, and, most importantly, what your values are. When you know your values, then you know your value. That is when you know the sound of your own heart. And you will be ready to start leading from a new, much-needed perspective.

To know what your driving story is, you need to delve deeply. You need to understand the answers to some very profound questions. These questions include the following: *What motivates you? What are your values? What do you stand for? What won't you stand for?*

To give you a sense of how personal this journey is, I am going to start by sharing with you what I discovered to be my driving story. This is at the very heart of defining who I am. I am being completely personal, open, and vulnerable with you because that is at the heart of my message: *connect with your heart, so you can connect with the hearts of others.*

MY DRIVING STORY

My story begins with disappointing my father. Then not being able to talk with him about it. I have come to realize that this one event at age sixteen fundamentally changed the way I have thought about myself ever since. Throughout my life, this memory has been like a shadow that I glimpse for a moment, out of the corner of my eye, following me around, constantly reminding me of the past. And I have had to outrun it. That moment organizes my life into a "before" and "after." It is at the heart of who I am.

My story begins back on March 19, 1974, when I was a junior at Cretin High School in St. Paul, Minnesota. Cretin was an all-boys Catholic school as well as a military academy—a double dose of discipline for us boys. This is the same school where my father went. When he graduated, he was a lieutenant colonel, which was second only to the cadet colonel in the school's military command. He intended to fight in World War II, but, because of his epilepsy, he was labeled 4F and could not enlist. Not being able to go to war when all his friends were there left a hole in my father's heart. He felt left behind, not where he needed to be, useless, and irrelevant. And there was absolutely nothing he could do.

So, twenty-seven years later, when I entered Cretin High School, my dad put his heart and soul into preparing me to be the cadet colonel. My father wanted me to have the accomplishment and the title that he never achieved. And I wanted it just as much.

We were extremely close. He had big dreams for me. And I wanted to live up to those dreams. We spent a lot of time together—lifting weights, playing handball, and sharing stories. On Saturdays we would go to the St. Paul Athletic Club together, where we would work out all day.

I was on the right trajectory to be the cadet colonel for the class of 1975. Everything I was doing academically, in sports, in the military training, and in service to our community was preparing me for that title, which we both knew could open up enormous opportunities for me in college and afterward. And I was being recruited by the air force, where I was going to play football.

This was when the country was bitterly divided over the Vietnam War. It was a time of enormous turmoil, ferment, and unrest. There were impassioned antiwar demonstrations in the streets with draft cards being burned. Meanwhile, I was at a military academy, founded by the Christian Brothers in 1871, honoring a deep sense of tradition, where we all had short hair and wore military dress uniforms every day with collared shirts and ties. We were part of one of the very first Junior ROTC programs in the country, so we learned how to stand at attention, march in command, and shoot rifles. We had inspection every Monday. Our uniforms, the brass on our belts, our shoes, our haircuts, the knots in our ties—everything was inspected. So, between the Christian Brothers and the military officers, there was round-the-clock preparation, discipline, and order. This training helped me to focus with clarity on my values. And I felt a deep connection with my father, as the tradition was being passed on to another generation.

In the spring of my junior year of high school, I was selected among the top leaders of my class to take a comprehensive military exam. The exam was pass–fail. If you scored an 87 or above, you passed. If you scored an 86 or below, you failed. Since it covered three years of cumulative military knowledge, I figured there was no way to study for it. But I felt amply prepared.

As it turned out, my parents were on vacation in Mexico the week I was taking the exam. So, my father called on Tuesday and asked how the test went.

"I don't know," I replied. "I think I did well. They say we'll know for sure tomorrow."

"Great," he said, then assured me he would call the next day. Even with the phone line fading in and out, I could hear the excitement in his voice. Of course, we did not have cell phones back then; he was calling from a pay phone in the tiny town of Cuernavaca, Mexico, with a spotty connection.

The next morning, I found out I got an 86. I'd failed. Any hope of me becoming a cadet colonel was dashed. There was nothing more I could do . . . except to wait for my father's call. And I can still hear the anticipation in his voice, as he asked, "How did it go?"

I was so embarrassed to tell him. I waited a moment to respond. Then I told him that I'd failed. I'd gotten an 86—missing a passing grade by one point.

He was devastated. Absolutely devastated. And I was devastated because I had disappointed him, and myself. It wasn't that he was angry or upset, but I could just hear his dream fall through the cracks from the staticky sound on a phone 2,100 miles away. And there was nothing he or I could do about it.

It was over. Our dream was lost. He'd been looking for me to follow in his footsteps, and I'd tripped up. I'd failed. There was no way I could make it right.

What I did not know was that I would never speak with my father again.

As it turned out, the following day, while still in Mexico, he began to feel ill after having lunch, and he was rushed to the closest hospital. My mom called from the hospital to let me know that he was not doing well.

She then called my parents' dear friend Dr. Thomas Votel, my dad's best friend since ninth grade. Dr. Tom, as I grew up calling him, later recalled that he was talking with my mom when someone shouted for her to rush over.

Fifteen minutes later, my mom called again—to tell me that my dad had died.

Later, Dr. Tom had pathologists at the Mayo Clinic and Mount Sinai try to determine what had happened to my dad, "but they could not come up with anything conclusive," he said. "All they could confirm was that he was very toxic."

The Monday after my father died, I went to the St. Paul Athletic Club and sat in front of my dad's locker, devastated. Then I opened his locker and put on his tennis shoes, and put on the gloves he wore to hit the heavy bag. I can still see his locker number, 747. It is so strange what you remember. Boom. Welcome to the new reality.

The final phone conversation with my father, when I told him that I hadn't passed the exam, was the last time my father and I ever spoke. Except for in my mind, we never got to talk again. The last sound I heard in his voice was disappointment. And it has echoed for my entire life.

I have been haunted by the last conversation I had with my father. I have played it over and over again.

And I am equally haunted by the conversations I never got to have with my father afterward.

All I needed was one more lousy point on that test. Which question did I get wrong? I just needed to get one more right. Then my life would have been different. At least the last words in this world that my father would have heard from me would not have disappointed him. I would have gone to the US Air Force Academy. I would have come through for my dad. I would have made him proud. And I could have believed more in myself.

For a long time, the only person I could talk to about this was my wife, Barb. And, in quiet moments, she would ask me, "What do you really think your father would have said if you were able to have the conversation with him that you never got to have?"

And I would respond that I did not know. I could not even imagine.

Then she would ask, "From everything I have heard about your father, can you imagine him putting his arm around you, and saying something like, 'I know that was hard. And that it hurts. But you'll get over it. What matters is . . . what are you going to do next?'" Then she would add, "From all you've told me, I can't help but think that he would have said something along those lines."

And I would reply, "I can't even imagine what he would have said. I cannot even go there."

I wasn't able to imagine my father saying something awful and hurtful, but neither could I imagine him saying something comforting and inspiring. I was just stuck in that awful moment. It was like a wound that could not heal. I'd really disappointed him. I'd killed our dream.

And so, somewhere in the back of my mind this unexpressed pain took various shapes and sizes, but never went away. The shadow of that pain was worse than any of my fears, as it seeped in and darkened my thoughts about who I was. My dad was not there any longer to put his arm around my shoulder—when I needed it most. Although, as if in a distance, through a fog, I can still see him, as tough as nails, leaning in toward me as if about to say something, with his piercing blue eyes, and his bald, shaven head like Yul Brynner's, shrugging his broad shoulders, looking dapper as always in one of his dress hats, which he wore 365 days a year.

My failure on that test has driven me my entire life. It has had a profound effect on me. I have spent the rest of my life trying—in so many ways—never to disappoint or fail my father again.

There has not been a day that has gone by from that point on—whether I was in college, or at my first job, or when I was president of Avis Budget Group—when I have not woken up and said, "Will my dad be proud of me today?"

That fear of failure has defined me and driven me.

But, then again, life can work in mysterious ways. Because if I had become the cadet colonel, I would have gone into the US Air Force Academy. Instead, I stayed in St. Paul, went to the College of St. Thomas, met my wife, got married and had kids, and my career took off. I have had a beautiful life, been very fortunate, worked hard, and (knock on wood) things have been very good. Still, such events in our lives become pivotal. And defining.

WHAT IS LEARNED?

For me, the drive to prove myself to my father is still central to who I am. Both early on and as I have continued my leadership journey, it drove me in ways that I was not even aware of.

One thing I learned—about myself and about life—is that the same experience can provide us with more than one important lesson as we reflect upon it at different times in our lives. The real turning point in my becoming a leader that others wanted to follow came much later in my career. As I said, I wish I knew it earlier. But, like so many of life's lessons, it took me a while to catch on.

That change came when I shifted from needing to prove myself to my father to wanting to share what I had learned from him. And among the most important things I had learned from him was how to have open, honest, and encouraging conversations with everyone I cared about. Just like the talks that he and I used to have as we worked out in the gym. Or when he came home from work. Or if I was struggling with a situation at school.

I knew I needed to have open conversations with people, to start sharing my life stories, including this story about my dad and its effects on me. I had kept this story inside of me for too long. I'd carried it around almost like a shield, and then I realized it could no longer protect me. In fact, keeping this story to myself had never protected me. I needed to let the light in. So I began to open up.

That shift, for me, was enormous. It was fundamental to connecting my head with my heart, and fundamental to me becoming more of who I am—personally and professionally. Once the shift occurred, all I knew for certain was that *I wanted to lead in a way where I was much more open about sharing what was in my heart—and I was much*

*more interested in discovering what was in the hearts of those
around me.*

That is how I realized that my journey into leadership
had begun with this overwhelming need to prove who I was
to my dad—or, more so, to my memory of him. Then, after
I learned to accept myself, as he always did (though I'd lost
sight of that along the way), I took in more completely the
lessons he had been teaching me all along—most importantly, to be more open and to connect more deeply with
others. Taking this to heart allowed me to grow as a leader,
and it became my first and most important lesson in learning to lead with heart.

My desire is for you to be able to learn to lead with your
heart, too. That is why I have shared my deeply personal
story with you. I have been so open with you because it gets
to the heart of who I am. My fervent hope is that by opening
myself up like this it helps you to open up to the depth and
meaning of your own story, so that your leadership journey
can take hold.

My dream is that together we can create a new paradigm
for what it truly takes to lead—which is recognizing that
true leadership begins inside of each of our hearts.

SO, WHAT ARE YOU AFRAID OF?

Ever since I got an 86 on that comprehensive exam, disappointing myself and my father, I have been afraid of failing.

This fear has been a primary motivating force in my life. I will do everything in my power *not* to fail—which means I prepare and prepare. Then I prepare again.

In some ways, this has caused me to redefine (at least for myself) the notion of being afraid to fail.

Traditionally, *fear of failure* is a psychological phrase that means being so afraid of failing that, subconsciously, we stop ourselves from taking a chance and giving something our all. We may keep ourselves from taking on a challenging project, or self-sabotage by procrastinating or just not following through with a goal. Or our worry about what others think might become so overwhelming that we keep ourselves from getting involved. Or we may be so much of a perfectionist that we never finish a project for fear that it will not be "perfect" enough. Such fears can become so overpowering that they freeze us in our tracks. They can even become debilitating, causing physical symptoms that prevent us from completing a project.

For me, rather than allowing the fear of failure to stop me from doing what is needed to achieve my goals, that fear actually mobilizes me. *This fear has driven me to destinies that I am not sure I would have reached without it.* A large part of that—make that a very large part—is because I never want to get an 86 again. Not even an 87.

What can you do to overcome your fear?

Some people overcome their fear of failure by learning to think more positively. Much research has been done on how we can change our behavior by first changing the way we think about our experiences, which changes the way we feel about ourselves and the world around us. Martin Seligman, the founder of the field known as positive psychology, reminds us that our *explanatory style* (how we explain events) makes a world of difference. What we believe sets the stage for what can happen.

Here's a little test that Seligman created: *How do you view negative things that happen? Are they happening to you? To everyone? Can you change them?*

Pessimists view negative things that happen as *just the way things are*. What are you going to do?

Optimists, however, typically view a negative event as something rare that will pass, nothing personal.

Meanwhile, if something positive happens, a pessimist will view it as nothing more than a fluke, a chance occurrence, or an unexpected coincidence.

Optimists, on the other hand, will view a positive event as something they helped to make happen and will be able to make happen again.

In both cases, pessimists and optimists receive what they believe.

As Seligman explained, "I used to believe that optimism was about how you thought about things in the past. What I know now is that optimists are people who believe more good things will happen in the future."

While I have always considered myself to be optimistic, and I view the world as being full of opportunities, I also do everything I possibly can to make sure that things turn out positively. I embark on every new undertaking believing I will succeed. But I also plan for the future, then prepare with a fierce determination. I do not take anything for granted. I go over it all in my mind, again and again. I know that such planning will get me where I need to be. Because somewhere in the back of my mind is that painful memory of getting an 86. And I never want to experience that terrible sinking feeling again.

So, I have learned to take the energy from that fear and turn it into a driving, positive force as I clarify my goals, visualize attaining them, analyze potential outcomes, and create plans, along with contingency plans.

I remember when I surpassed my sales plan the first year I was an entry-level salesperson at Ecolab. At first, I was ecstatic. Then, after celebrating with my wife, I got this sinking feeling, as I started thinking about the coming year's plan. I felt queasy, as though I was rocking in a boat, lost at sea. How would I possibly be able to exceed this new plan? What if I failed? Such thoughts and feelings overcame me.

So, I started planning. And the more I planned, the less I worried.

I believe that my fear of failure—whether as an entry-level salesperson or as the leader of a company—is the drive behind my need to constantly plan and to have contingency plans. If I anticipated problems and created solutions far in advance, I felt, then the problems would become smaller. And if the possible problems never materialized, then the mitigation created additional revenue and profits.

To make those fears shrink, I first taught myself to visualize a half-year ahead, planning out the steps between now and then. After a while, I learned to see further into the future, visualizing what a year looked like down the road.

This approach to planning informed the way I would lead, whether at JohnsonDiversey or Avis. To meet each upcoming plan, I was always intent on having the pipeline full, and on converting new customers well ahead of revenue expectations.

What I eventually learned to do was to face my fears. And to see them as nothing more than my own shadow, lurking in the darkness.

That was when I learned to ease up and enjoy our successes in the moment—although I was still always building the pipeline for tomorrow.

My goal was to exceed my plan. I always strove to be ahead of the game. That is how my fear of failure drove me and helped me make sure that my failure was always in the rearview mirror.

My fear of failure also drove me to work harder, to surround myself with driven, compassionate, caring people, and together to search continuously for solutions to problems before they occurred.

Rather than stifle or hold me back, my fear of failure eventually pushed me beyond what I otherwise might have believed was possible.

Understanding your fears, I believe, is central to understanding your leadership potential.

I encourage you to ask yourself the following questions. And do not let yourself off the hook until you have wrestled your fears to the ground.

What are you really afraid of?
What worries never seem to go away?
How do you respond to failure?
What happens when you feel the sting of rejection?
How do you respond when things do not go your way?
How do you react to life's inevitable setbacks?
Do such experiences make you pull back? Or step up?

My very strong advice is to face your fear. Do not give it the power to make you look down. Do not look away from it. Look straight at it and embrace it. Understand it. Recognize it for what it is: a part of you that you may not have been ready to face when you were younger. But you are ready now. Then allow that energy to fuel you—and drive you to places you have never been before.

KNOWING THE SOUND OF YOUR OWN HEART: QUESTIONS FOR SELF-EVALUATION

The questions we ask ourselves, and how deeply we answer them, help to shape who we become. With that in mind, I encourage you to dive deeply as you explore these questions. Then review your answers from time to time. And allow your answers to evolve. Your answers will serve as road signs on your leadership journey.

1. Do you know what experiences have had the most profound effect on who you are—and on who you will become?

2. How has that experience shaped who you are personally?

3. How has that experience enabled you to understand your deeper purpose as a leader?

4. How comfortable are you at sharing your transformative story?

5. How can you become even more comfortable sharing your story?

6. How is your story motivating you to achieve at higher levels, to become a top performer, to constantly keep pushing yourself?

7. What do you have to prove? To yourself? To others? To the memory of someone who is no longer here?

8. What have you learned about yourself by facing your most difficult challenge?
9. Where you are going?
10. How you will get there?

CHAPTER 3

OPENING YOURSELF UP—
TO YOURSELF AND TO OTHERS

Part of the impetus for changing my thoughts and feelings about how I wanted to lead came from accepting a position as the executive vice president of sales and marketing for Avis Budget Group. Taking on this new position meant that my wife, Barb, and I had to uproot ourselves from the St. Paul area, where we'd grown up, raised our family, and had many friends who were all very dear to us. While there would be much to do in and around the metropolitan New York area where we were moving, I knew that leaving our friends and family would create a void in our lives. I wanted to make sure that Barb felt a vital part of everything I was doing.

I saw this move to a new environment as an opportunity for me to "show up" in a new way, to be a different kind of leader than I'd been. I wanted to lead in a way that integrated my personal life with my professional life. I made a conscious decision to *reinvent myself* as a leader. I would consider the messages underlying everything I did and said.

So, in many ways, moving to this new organization in this new part of the country allowed me the freedom to lead in a way that was truer to myself than how I had led in the past. It gave me the opportunity to explore my newfound desire, which, I had yet to understand, would become how I would learn to *lead with heart*.

One of the first things I did, since I knew I was going to pour my heart and soul into succeeding in this new position, was to make sure that Barb was included as much as possible. That helped me to change my message about what is important in life. That was how I began to recreate who I was as a leader.

"FAMILY FIRST" BECAME MY MOTTO

I started thinking and feeling about families in a new way. I was looking for something beyond just work/life balance. I wanted to know the families of the people I was working with. And I wanted them to know Barb and me on a personal level. For our connections to be real, I felt, they had to be deep. I wanted to be more open about what was in my heart—and even more, I wanted to discover what was in the hearts of those around me.

So as I began this new role, I was most interested in strengthening the connections between our families at home and our families at work.

It started with my concept of "family" broadening. It wasn't just that I and those I worked with were getting to know each other's families. *I came to believe that we were all part of an extended family.* And I wanted our "work family" to be there for each other, just like our home family.

Central to my message about family was that everybody was equally important in our organization—regardless of what role they played. We are all in it together, I emphasized and demonstrated.

There were times when the people who quickly fixed a problem with a car that had been recalled saved our bacon. There were other times when the person helping the customer was the hero. Still other times, a salesperson bringing in a brand-new client was the most important person. My message was that there were times when we could each become the most important person in our company. Who is most important changes every day, depending upon what is going on. What matters is that we all feel that sense of family, that we are all in it together, and that we recognize how vital we all are to each other's success.

"Family First" became my motto. And as I started saying it often, this message started to resonate with those around me in ways that were very refreshing.

This was important to me—make that *very important*—because earlier in my career, as I was pursuing my goals, I knew that there had been many times when I was absent as a father. And I was keenly aware of the toll that can take on a family. So, I took this opportunity to realize my commitment to leading with my heart. From here on, I would be personally committed to leading in an organization where I could embrace my heartfelt belief that the demands of success must never outweigh the importance of family.

Through this new role, I allowed myself to open up and grow into a way of leading that was, for me, truly transformational. By being more open, I discovered, I was helping to create a culture of trust, understanding, togetherness, and collaboration. The added benefit, which I was thrilled to realize, was that I was also helping to create a culture whose very pulse was connected to each of our hearts.

The heart of my message evolved into a much more compassionate view of what an organization could become.

Once we created a feeling of family within the company, it was only natural for us all to become much more concerned about the families of those with whom we were working. But I am getting ahead of myself.

The point I want to emphasize is that this change, for me, started in simple ways. And some of those new ways I began to lead were easy and fun. For instance, one of the first things I did was to invite our management team, their spouses, and their children to the office for a breakfast early in December—and I dressed up as Santa Claus. It was just a way to break the ice, have fun, and let them know (while I reminded myself) that I was going to lead in a new way. We were going to take our work seriously—but not ourselves. I also made sure that spouses were invited to events in which we shared our plans for the future and celebrated our successes. It set a clear tone that we were all in it together.

Those experiences allowed me to connect with people in ways that were very deep and personal.

LOWERING THE DRAWBRIDGE

As I got to know my collaborators better, I found myself becoming much more open to sharing on a very personal level what was happening in my life. This was when I began to openly share with my colleagues that one of our children needed help to overcome an addiction. Once Barb and I realized how serious the addiction had become, I disclosed that we sought treatment for our child at the Hazelden Betty Ford Foundation. This was a time of excruciating pain and startling realizations for all of us as a family.

Among our many unexpected realizations, we learned that my wife and I were both enablers. With the best of intentions, we had made excuses for our child, trying to solve all the problems that were being created, while eliminating the consequences of the negative behavior. And in so doing, we discovered we were not providing our child with the sense of personal responsibility needed to come to terms with those mistakes and make the changes necessary to face reality. It was very difficult, I openly shared, for us to realize that we were inadvertently contributing to our child's addiction by trying to cover up and brush aside those mistakes.

We were full of so many conflicting feelings, including guilt, helplessness, and an overriding sense that we had somehow failed as parents. We learned that talking about these overwhelming feelings was helpful for us and for others. Sharing what we were going through was much healthier and more helpful than acting as if, or pretending that, everything was "just fine."

As I shared with my colleagues how my wife and I were learning to stop enabling our child, it was not unusual for people to start crying. I believe that those tears started to fall because my openness and vulnerability touched people in unexpected ways. And through my being so open, it also allowed them to open up—often in ways that they had never even considered, particularly in a business setting. I also came to realize that it is more common than not for someone in every family to be encountering a serious problem, if not a crisis. Often, though, I came to understand that people can be reluctant to talk about their personal difficulties for myriad reasons.

I learned that by opening myself up, I was actually providing those around me with an enormous opportunity. It allowed them to get in touch with their own feelings. It allowed all of us to create much deeper connections with each other. And it helped me become a leader whom people were more interested in following.

For instance, when I first met my former colleague Andre Meesschaert, whom I eventually promoted to a senior position, I was genuinely interested in knowing more about him. My intuition told me he had enormous potential. I had just traveled to Toronto for my first business review, in which I politely, but in a very direct manner, let the team know that the organization's sales performance was not what I expected. "Our meetings tended to be very polite in a Canadian kind of way," Andre said. "But Tom cut through all of that."

After the meeting, Andre offered to drive me to the airport. We had just resolved several major decisions, but rather than review those with him, which I could easily do over the phone later, I wanted to use our time together to get to know Andre better—and for him to get to know me.

As Andre recalled, "Our first conversation became very personal and open—at a level that I was not used to from someone in a senior position like him."

He said he initially found my being so candid to be disarming. Then he realized that, for me, there was a time for directness in a business setting, and a time for openness in a personal conversation. Andre said he had "never come across that combination before in one person," and that it opened him up to new possibilities in what it meant to be a leader.

How did our conversation connect so deeply and become so memorable for Andre? Rather than ask him some probing questions about his background and aspirations, which he could have found intimidating, I started off by telling him some personal stories about myself and my family. Now, of course, I recognize that there are some leaders who are consumed with their own stories. So, after telling a story about themselves, they turn to another story about themselves, or just change the subject to something about business.

What I am suggesting is something quite different. For me, sharing a personal story about myself is just the first step in opening up and being curious about whoever I am with. This approach to connecting involves equal parts of sharing your story and genuinely caring to hear about someone else's story. The effect of opening myself up is that it quickly lowers the drawbridge between whoever I am with and me. Then, I allow them to open themselves up—to whatever extent they feel comfortable. That is where the opening occurs for a deep and abiding level of trust to be established. And once the trust is there, a world of new possibilities begins to occur.

So after I opened up with Andre about my own stories, he felt comfortable sharing stories with me about himself and his family. As Andre said, "It became clear that Tom cared about me. Then, over time, that care for me and my family became deep and abiding. That is the kind of leader you are willing to go through anything for. There is a positive attachment that binds you to such a leader."

Opening yourself up, I have found, not only lowers the drawbridge, but is also the first step in creating trust and a deep connection among those with whom you work. For others to trust you, they need to know who you are. They want to know what is inside of you.

This is echoed by Baron Carlson, a partner in AEA, a leading global private investment firm, where I am currently a senior advisor. "Far too many business people put up walls," he noted. "They keep the interaction strictly on a business level. So, when you walk away, you can be left with a bland feeling. Even if you had a perfectly constructive conversation, you do not feel like you know that person any better. With Tom, you get to know him more each time you talk with him. That is a fundamental distinction."

He described my tendency to tear up in conversations: "Tom will get emotional, on a personal level, in a positive way, when he is telling a story about someone he cares about deeply." He added, "I am still moved when I remember him telling me about how he and his wife were praying at the hospital for their grandson Tommy, who was born at twenty-seven weeks, weighing just a little more than one and a half pounds. He allowed me to see inside his world. And that tells me that he is someone who has depth and substance."

"When we spoke the next time," Baron noted, "while I was seeking his advice about the performance of a company, the first thing I wanted to know was how his grandson was doing. And I am thrilled and amazed to hear how well he continues to do."

Baron paused, then said, "When Tom shares, he invites you to share. Then something inside of you opens up. If you are going to have that kind of relationship—where you can have a frank conversation about what is going on in your life—it can create an openness and a level of trust that can affect your next conversation, which may just be about a quick business decision you need to make together. What matters most is the trust that is there. It is all about opening up to that depth."

OPENING UP—*PERSONALLY*
AND PROFESSIONALLY

I have come to believe that once you become comfortable being open with your colleagues, you can seamlessly shift between personal and professional conversations. That, I believe, is when you are being true—to yourself and to others. This is all about opening yourself up personally and professionally. To me, there really is no difference. That ability to be open is what makes life much more interesting.

By way of example, when I first joined Avis, Pat Siniscalchi, who was at the helm of international operations for the organization, and I made a pact to share the feedback from our 360 assessments with each other. Pat and I were very open and honest with each other, which created a deep bond and sense of trust. As a result, we grew together in ways that we would not have otherwise.

As we were going through a leadership training course together, taught by Linkage, we openly shared the feedback we were getting and explored together how we might look at each of our own developments differently. We had several lengthy conversations about how each of us could improve. And those discussions created a level of understanding that continuously grew deeper.

We both agreed to take one or two things that we really wanted to improve on and help each other uncover ways to reach our desired results. This took an enormous amount of trust.

So, Pat coached me on how I could sometimes, without intending it, intimidate others. As he explained, "Tom is almost like a bigger-than-life-figure. So, I coached him on how to ease up and listen more. And in the three years he was at the company, I saw his ability to relate with people in every aspect of our organization improve dramatically."

Through a new lens, Pat helped me to recognize and accept certain aspects of my leadership style, while I changed others.

So, while I was not willing to decelerate the speed at which I intended to accomplish our objectives, I was willing to slow down personally and bring people along. I learned to be more patient as I explained my thoughts to others and listened to their perspective.

Ultimately, Pat's counsel—as well as the fresh, trusting, in-depth, and open approach we took toward collaborating with each other—helped us both become better leaders in ways that were transformative.

Interestingly, the key area that I coached Pat on was also how to listen more openly to advice. But the advice for Pat came from a different perspective. As he said, "Because I thought I was working in a part of the business that most people did not understand, I would get impatient with their advice. To me, their ideas seemed to miss some very important cultural nuances. Through the 360 feedback and Tom's coaching, I realized that my attitude was creating some resentment. So, I had to come to terms with that, and become more open in my approach to listening and leading."

Pat also shared that he realized he needed help in how he was presenting to the board. "I knew that I was not as effective as I wanted to be," he said. "But I was not sure what to do. Tom was very helpful with his advice in coaching me, which many colleagues will shy away from. He counseled me on how to focus on what was important without getting lost in the specifics. I would illustrate three points from Canada, three points from New Zealand, and three points from Mexico. Tom helped me to change my attitude, my approach, and my messages when I was presenting to the board—so that I was much more focused on what was important. In addition, rather than highlight what we could do better, he helped me to also emphasize our successes, and our aspirations."

After Pat and I coached each other on what we had gleaned from our 360 evaluations, I called my team together and shared with them all my feedback. Gina Bruzzichesi, who was the senior vice president of strategic customer leadership at the time, recalled, "Tom did not just talk about his results; he actually gave all of us a copy of his 360 evaluation. I had never seen any leader be so completely transparent. He shared what was positive and what he intended to work on. And he wanted to know from all of us what he could do to become a better leader. I have never come across a leader with such an unusual combination of being so driven *and* so vulnerable."

From a copy of my 360 evaluation that she still has, Gina explained that it had comments in six different areas: *Focused Drive, Trusted Influence, Conceptual Thinking, Leadership Skills, Communication Style,* and *Leading Teams.*

Of the faults, she said, "One comment was, *'It is import-ant to note that while you ask great questions, you can come across as not being interested in the answer. Sometimes people feel as though you already have the solution in your head.'* That, Tom said, is something I am definitely going to work on. Another comment was: *'You tend to lose patience with people who don't show the same level of commitment as you demonstrate.'* And another was: *'Tom has a very defined vision for what it means to be part of a team. He reacts nega-tively to what he perceives as whining and complaining.'* Those last two comments are accurate reflections of who I am,' he said, then assured us, 'and those I will never change.'"

Gina added, "The report also went on to say that Tom *'does what he says he is going to do'* and *'unfalteringly expects the same of others,'* that when he hears the word *'no,'* he just assumes *'they haven't got it yet,'* that he is *'intense,'* is *'extraor-dinarily decisive,'* an *'aggressive change agent,'* and that *'there is no question Tom will tell you what is on his mind.'*" It also said, "*he could be more patient with others' perspectives, can over-schedule himself, wants 'Rome built in a day,'* and *'needs to keep strong, trusted, process-oriented people on his team to act as a check for his speed-to-action bias.'*"

After sharing with my team everything that was written, I thanked them all for their honesty, telling them how much I appreciated their compliments in certain areas and letting them know that I was very grateful for their advice in other aspects of how I was leading.

Then, after reviewing each area, I asked for them to freely share with me their thoughts and feelings about how I could become a better leader. In a very open, wide-ranging, hour-long conversation, I made commitments to them that I was going to improve on some of the shortcomings that had been highlighted. And I asked them to let me know, over the course of time, how I was doing.

Most importantly, I learned, and was demonstrating, not only how to open myself up, sharing honestly and very openly, but how to communicate the worth of each person, to convey that their input is valuable. I was modeling how I completely believed in those with whom I chose to surround myself.

Gina said, "I found this experience to be so valuable—because of how vulnerable Tom was. He said, 'Here's what you guys are saying about me. And I want you to help me to become a better leader.' And it was a very honest conversation. I have taken this as a real learning experience. I have taken this same approach with my team ever since, and it has helped me to become a much better leader. And like Tom's team, the members of my team initially said that they had never had a leader do that before. It is so refreshing, I've been told time and again, to be part of such a very honest way of leading people."

She added, "I thank Tom for encouraging and allowing me to be that kind of leader. He got to know me. He wanted to know what was important to me. He cared that I wanted to have a baby. And he encouraged me in creating a path to eventually heading up a company. He wanted to know who I was—my concerns and my dreams. For him it all starts with wanting to know you personally. A lot of leaders do not go there. I know and appreciate how rare that is. He invited my family to his home. When my first child was born, he and his wife, Barb, came to Hoboken to help me set things up. I have Barb's cell phone number on my phone, just like I have Tom's."

She paused, then added, "He introduced me to an entirely different way of leading—one which starts by truly caring. That allowed me to take my leadership ability to the next level with confidence—because I saw how he treated me and my family. And I became much more comfortable doing that with the people on my team. Since then, I have invited my team and their spouses to dinner, gotten to know them personally, and I have become much more comfortable expressing how I truly care about what is going on in their lives."

Opening yourself up is the necessary ingredient to establishing trust. Then, showing that you truly care about someone—about their sorrows and their joys—is where the seeds are planted for a truly meaningful personal connection. And, I have learned, there really is no difference between opening myself up personally and opening myself up professionally. It is all the same. It is about being real.

Ultimately, when you connect who you are personally with who you are professionally, you open yourself up to having more honest, meaningful, and deep relationships with those around you. And it creates a quantum leap in building trust, understanding, and collaboration.

By opening yourself up, you are opening up to new possibilities—for you as a leader and for your organization's future.

AS AN EMERGING LEADER, YOU NEED A BOSS WHO BELIEVES IN YOU

I was in an environment that was conducive to my opening myself up—and I had a boss in Ron Nelson, then the chairman and chief executive officer, who was very trusting and supportive. Without Ron's backing, I never could have made the leadership changes I desired. I am very grateful to him. And I am very glad that I took advantage of the opportunities he afforded me to lead in a new way.

Interestingly, Ron said, "I brought Tom on because I was looking for succession candidates. He had P&L experience, which I liked about him. But most importantly, what I liked most about him was his values."

Ron, who had also worked in Hollywood as the co–chief operating officer of DreamWorks, added, "I told the board that the reason I wanted to bring him on to head up sales and marketing was because he reminded me of Tom Cruise in the movie *All the Right Moves.* In that movie, Tom is the son of a steel mill worker in a depressed small town. He has a chance at a football and academic scholarship. But he assumes responsibility for his family. I saw those qualities in Tom. I was inspired by the strength of his character, and by his values."

Ron recognized, as he said, that "when Tom became president, it brought out and gave him an opportunity to show what he really had. From the outside, it might have looked like he changed as he became president. But I believe the opportunity provided him with the chance to become more of himself. He needed that opportunity to showcase those qualities."

I was very fortunate to have a boss like Ron who believed in me and allowed me to lead in my own way.

This brings up a cautionary note: if you are not in an environment that supports you opening up to your true leadership potential, then the unfortunate truth is that your potential will not be realized. Instead, you will feel like you are trying to defy gravity. My strong advice to anyone who finds themselves in a stifling relationship with their boss or stuck in a stagnant environment is to get out and find another place to lead. Because without that support, your professional growth will be put on hold. Or worse, shifted into reverse.

But with that support, your leadership possibilities are only limited by your own imagination and your desire to open up to new possibilities.

OPENING YOURSELF UP—TO YOURSELF AND TO OTHERS: QUESTIONS FOR SELF-EVALUATION

The questions we ask ourselves, and how deeply we answer them, help to shape who we become. With that in mind, I encourage you to dive deeply as you explore these questions. Then review your answers from time to time. And allow your answers to evolve. Your answers will serve as road signs on your leadership journey.

1. How many people are you "open" to within your organization?
2. Who would you like to be more open with? When will you become more open with that person?
3. Who will the next person after that be?
4. Is there a deep level of trust, honesty, and openness in your organization?
5. If so, how can you increase it?
6. If not, are you in the right place?

CHAPTER 4

BUILDING AN ENGAGED, TRUSTING CULTURE

One of my favorite questions to ask other leaders is, "When you have a difficult decision to make, how many people do you usually talk with about it?" One leader told me, "There are three people I can talk with in complete confidence." Another quickly added that he had five people he could talk with "in complete confidence."

I thought that was interesting. Because that was not the question I asked. I did not ask, "Who can you talk with in complete confidence?" Rather, I simply asked, "When you have a difficult decision to make, how many people do you usually talk with about it?"

The answer to that question for me is easy. I will talk with as many people as I possibly can to get as many viewpoints as possible. And I respect each and every one of those perspectives. Perhaps it is because I worked in a steel fabricating plant while I was going to college at night, but I respect the opinions of everyone on the ground, working close to the problems, as much as I respect the viewpoints of outside advisors and board members. And I respect the perspective of someone who was just hired as much as I respect the ideas of someone who has been with the organization for their entire career.

For me, it is all about connecting. And each of those connections is grounded in trust. When I talk to as many people as possible about a decision, not only do I get a wide variety of viewpoints that can assist me in what call to make, but the very act of being open, sharing myself with those around me, and being genuinely interested, can create an uncommon bond of trust.

Trust is the true measure of the strength of any relationship. Ironically, however, so many leaders view trust as a rare quality—like an invaluable gem that they keep safely locked up and only take out on rare occasions, as a privilege for just a chosen few to experience.

I have seen far too many leaders who believe that trust can only go so far. So, they choose to trust just a small cadre of confidants. Those confidants become part of their inner circle. This tight-knit group becomes known as their "trusted advisors." That, then, becomes the extent of their trust. Everyone else is kept at a safe distance, fanning out from that close and closed circle, getting only hints and glimpses of what is behind the curtain. After a while, not surprisingly, such leaders come to discover that they have lost touch with their organization, their clients, and the marketplace.

I understand where this misguided understanding of trust comes from. I was once that way myself. Because of this, I understand that leaders who limit their trust are really acting out of fear. They are following that unwritten rule of not getting too close to those they lead. And, without realizing it, these disconnected leaders are instilling a foundation of distrust within their organizations.

I surround myself *only* with people whom I trust completely, but the difference is I am trusting, and I prefer to build a relationship with the belief that we are all trustworthy. Instead of letting fear lead, I let love and trust lead. I assume we can trust each other—unless you prove otherwise.

So when I meet a new person, I start out being open and vulnerable, which leads to trust. I allow that to happen, without any expectations. With that foundation of trust, I am always asking questions—and listening. I am always listening for the truth. And it often surprises me. And leads me in new directions. For me, that is how trust leads to truth.

But again, if that trust is violated, we are done.

FOUR PRINCIPLES FOR BUILDING A TRUSTING CULTURE

To help build a trusting culture, I started sharing with everyone in our organization four of my core beliefs—my guiding principles, which began to connect us all in ways that ran clear and deep. I believe they connected with people because they spoke to their hearts.

FAMILY FIRST

The first guiding principle I shared was that I believe in *Family First*. I want those I work with to know that I care about them *and* their families. And I want them to feel the same about each other. I let them know that I am committed to them, with the implicit assumption that they are committed to their careers and to our company, and that we all treat those we are working with as part of our extended family.

When I say *Family First* it takes on two meanings. First and foremost, as I mentioned in chapter two, it is about your family at home, those you love and care about and whose bond connects you together in ways that run deep, often with rich traditions that have gone on for generations. Then, equally important for the culture we were trying to create, I wanted everyone to start considering the people we worked with as part of their family. After all, we are often spending more time with each other than we are with our families at home. Why not feel the strength and warmth of those connections? If not, I came to see, we were all missing out. At its best, our business could become an extension of our families. As this feeling turned into a commitment, it became my rallying cry.

As a result, I came to know that the people around me were there for me, and they knew that I was there for them in the same way. Through good times and bad times, through our peaks, valleys, and plateaus, we were sharing a commitment with each other that was becoming deep and visceral. The culture we were creating together dismantled any kind of hierarchy and any focus on ego. It created an understanding of humility and integrity. And people were drawn to it naturally. We also knew that this feeling we were creating separated us from our competition. And our customers could feel it as well.

WORKING HALF-DAYS

In addition, I would start to explain to everyone why you only need to *Work Half-Days* to succeed. Then, with a smile, I would quickly add, "That means twelve-hour days." While they knew I was kidding, the underlying message was to give it your all. I expected everyone to be committed fully. It is not about punching a clock. It is a state of mind. It is about going the extra mile and coming through for each other, for our customers, and for our company—so we can all succeed.

That is why I have come to believe that the elusive concept of "work/life balance" is not really about balancing at all. I believe it is about blending, harmonizing, and understanding. If you are looking to advance your career, you need a high level of commitment. And, sometimes, that leaves little room for work/life balance. What it does take is a mutual understanding between individual contributors and their managers that they are in it together, committed, trying harder, giving it their all. Then, there are going to be times—whether to see a child's recital or because of an emergency—when family will come first. There is room for that, so long as there is the commitment and the understanding. That understanding creates the bond that connects people who are working together, knowing that they are there for each other, in it together.

Work/life balance, I believe, is really a matter of priorities, not just hours. That is why it is important to recognize what is in the heart and mind of each person with whom you are working. There are times when a looming deadline will make it so that you have to put in far more time at work than you expected, just as there are going to be times when your personal priorities will need to take precedence.

There are also going to be times to hit the pause button on your career. Certainly, when your child or parent or spouse needs care, your emphasis on work will take second place. Also, as many professionals reach the end of their careers, they may see priorities differently. An engaged leader is able to recognize this in others and create a space for them to thrive—*so long as they are still committed and caring.* So, jobs might be recreated to take advantage of an individual's talents as their personal needs change. Those changes might be temporary. And that's okay. An effective leader needs to do the right thing for the company *and* for the individual. Ideally, those two aspects of the right thing can be found together.

WINNING

Then, along with emphasizing *Family First* and *Work Half-Days,* I shared with everyone my philosophy about

Winning. First and foremost, I let them know my firm belief that *we all can make a real difference.* If each of us improves a customer's experience in one new way today, then we, as a company, are going to succeed. It is about *doing the right thing for our customers.* Then, all of those little successes do not just add up. They multiply to create a huge and significant difference. Those "wins" create a truly caring culture, along with renewed revenue. We are all in a position to make a difference—whether solving a problem or creating a smile—to enhance the experience for our customers. And when our customers win, we all win. *We own it. Together.* That's how we all win.

WORDS PLUS ACTIONS MATCHING

The fourth guiding principle that I have learned for developing trust comes from a phrase that I repeat often: *Words Plus Actions Matching.* I first heard those words from Margaret Thompson, one of the counselors at Hazelden Betty Ford Foundation, a world-renowned rehabilitation center where one of our children and, therefore, our family, was treated. Margaret is a professional of enormous strength and conviction, who knows whereof she speaks, and she connects in ways that are admirable, honest, straightforward, and very helpful.

As Margaret explained, "One of the most fundamental aspects of addiction is that trust is broken. To me, addiction is about dishonesty. To maintain their use of a behavior or substance, addicts need to lie to their family and friends, who desperately want to believe them. But the addiction becomes paramount, so truth takes a backseat, and their words do not match their actions. I see dishonesty as a symptom of this disease. Telling the truth is at the heart of the cure. So, the formula I came up with for addicts and their families is that *Trust Equals Words Plus Actions Matching Over Time.*"

She added, "It all comes down to trust. And to trust you, I need to believe in you." It is that simple. And that complicated.

Ever since hearing that phrase—*Words Plus Actions Matching*—I apply it to everything I do—personally and professionally. When you say you are going to do something, follow through. When you make a commitment, live up to it. Be true to your word. That is our message. It is about having principles. Sticking to them. So, I have borrowed this phrase, which beautifully captures something I have always believed, and made it one of my key leadership tenets.

Now, in my personal life, this principle is what guides me. In a corporate setting, I see it as an essential part of the formula for creating a great culture—where we believe in each other and come through for each other—and for our customers.

What I have also come to realize is that by sharing my family's personal journey with those I am working with, it helps to create a greater level of trust and opens up new possibilities for our relationships to become even deeper.

As Margaret shared, "I wish everyone in the world could learn this way to live, that they could take these principles on and live by them."

That is why I openly tell people where I first heard the phrase *Words Plus Actions Matching*. And I openly share some insights I learned about helping people recover from addiction, which, interestingly, apply directly to how to create a culture of trust, engagement, collaboration, and innovation. And, inevitably, someone in the audience tells me about a personal experience—either their own or someone in their family—struggling to overcome an addiction. Then, together, we connect on a very deep level, realizing that we all have personal struggles that we are striving to rise above, and that we are all in this together.

What is the possible downside of having a fellowship of support, having a commitment to care about each other, being there in times of need, and then coming through for you as you come through for me?

While I was participating in the family program at the Hazelden Betty Ford Foundation, I could not help but think about what would happen on a major scale if we all started living with these philosophies.

To build trust begins with a very simple formula. First, say out loud what you are going to do. Then do it. Then repeat. Again. And again. That is how people will come to trust you. As you are doing what you say you will do, treat everyone with respect. And let them know that you have their best interest at heart.

TRUST YOUR HEART

My goal in being open and trusting those around me was to create a ripple effect that would ultimately start to change the culture of the organization. It started when I allowed myself to be the leader I wanted—and felt I needed—to be. For me, this was personal. From that point on, leading any other way would no longer work for me. I knew that I needed to feel the freedom of being open and the depth of being connected to those around me. And, equally important, I wanted to enable and encourage *all* of my team members to feel the same. It was very important to me that they, too, were able to feel open and vulnerable, so they could speak their unvarnished truth.

It all started with trust. And that trust, we were discovering together, became contagious—and led the way to our future. As Andre Meesschaert, one of our global leaders, shared, "This way of leading had never even occurred to me before. By being open and vulnerable with those around us, we began to experience an unwavering level of trust and true collaboration."

Together, we were learning how to feel connected to each other and open up to new possibilities. That is why trust needs to permeate everything you do if you are going to *lead with heart.*

I believe in trusting my instincts, and trusting people (unless, of course, they demonstrate that I should not trust them). Rather than "trusting your gut," as so many leaders like to say, I encourage you to trust your heart. Your heart is where trust does or does not reside.

For others to trust you, they need to know who you are. They want to know what is inside of you. Then they will believe that you can take them where they need to go.

WITHOUT TRUST, YOU WILL FAIL

While most people see me as being very confident and decisive, that does not mean that I do not doubt myself. I can question myself at any given moment. I reevaluate myself constantly, sometimes in my sleep. And I can challenge myself in the shower, before my first cup of coffee. Those questions, I have come to learn, keep me on track. Is there something I should be doing differently? Could I be doing it just a little better? Am I living up to my values? Most importantly, would my dad be proud of me?

Just ask my wife. I have these conversations with her (and myself) many times. But I do not let any of that stop me from pursuing what I believe to be true. I just use the questioning as a way to check in with myself. Then, when my internal scales tip in favor of a decision, I forge ahead.

As I shared with you from the beginning, "fear of failure" has driven me for most of my life. I firmly believe that fear, at times, and in just the right doses, can be a positive motivating force. It can be a much-needed wake-up call. It is often that kick in the butt that we need when, for instance, our competition introduces an innovative new product. Fear, at such times, can be the spark that ignites us. What matters is that we channel that fear into positive action.

That does not mean, however, that I am a fan of fear. I am keenly aware that when fear lingers it can have very negative consequences.

If you are working in a culture where fear is persistent and pervasive—dominating your heart and your mind—the results will be devastating. Such cultures will chip away at your very soul. I have seen such organizations crush people and destroy dreams, leaving the best of intentions scattered on the ground. People within companies that are fear based lose any sense that they could possibly win. With their confidence shaken, they feel like they are stuck, going nowhere—or worse, sliding backward. Focus becomes blurred as progress is sabotaged. People check, double-check, then triple-check their every move because they do not want to be blamed for making a wrong call. Meanwhile, whining, moaning, bickering, doubting, and finger-pointing seep in, destroying the foundation of trust upon which a successful organization needs to be built.

Whenever I walk into such fear-based organizations, I can feel it immediately. The negative energy is instantly depleting, and my immediate reaction is to want to turn around and walk out. I know that, like a ship without a rudder, such organizations are destined to fail and bring everyone down around them.

On the other hand, when I walk into organizations such as Southwest, and talk with leaders such as Dave Ridley, the airline's former chief marketing officer, I am immediately energized. Southwest's logo is a vibrant, tricolored heart. And everything about the organization is reflected by a classic line from one of their advertisements: "Without a heart, it's just a machine."

When you walk into Southwest's headquarters in Dallas, you can see that everything was designed to reflect the organization's core values: Warrior Spirit, Servant's Heart, and Fun-LUVing Attitude. (LUV is the NYSE symbol for Southwest Airlines.) As Dave said, "Those values are what we hire for. They are part of our performance appraisals. They permeate our culture."

In the Fun-LUVing Culture Center, which was inspired by Southwest's bigger-than-life cofounder, chairman emeritus, and former CEO, Herb Kelleher, they posted some of the actual things their flight attendants have said, including: *"Just sit back and enjoy the ride. Or you can sit up and be tense." "People, people, we're not picking out furniture here. Find a seat and get in it." "If you should get to use the life vest in a real-life situation, the vest is yours to keep."*

Love is the difference.

I have heard it said that the opposite of love is not hate; it is indifference. And I get that. I understand the difference between the fullness of love and the emptiness of indifference.

But I have also come to believe that the opposite of love may be fear. And an organization that runs on fear will cave in upon itself. Meanwhile, an organization with love will connect each of us together in ways that we would never have imagined, opening doors that we never knew existed, keeping us moving in positive, new directions—and deepening our bond of trust, allowing us and our organizations to flourish.

BUILDING AN ENGAGED, TRUSTING CULTURE: QUESTIONS FOR SELF-EVALUATION

The questions we ask ourselves, and how deeply we answer them, help to shape who we become. With that in mind, I encourage you to dive deeply as you explore these questions. Then review your answers from time to time. And allow your answers to evolve. Your answers will serve as road signs on your leadership journey.

1. Whom do you trust?
2. Who trusts you?
3. How deep is that trust?
4. Do you believe that trust and doubt are opposites?
5. Is trust for you an on-off switch? Or a dimmer switch?
6. What do you do when your trust has been broken?
7. Have you ever rebuilt trust?
8. Where do you get your best advice?

CHAPTER 5

SOMETIMES IT TAKES BEING FRIGGIN' CRAZY

When I became president, North America, of Avis Budget Group, I understood that our culture was full of people who were yearning to feel committed and make a difference. But we had twenty thousand people scattered across the United States and Canada. And I could sense they were feeling disconnected.

Our people were coming through for our customers. They were results oriented. But I felt that something was missing. There was no feeling of "us," no shared sense of purpose. We needed to find a way to connect with each other.

I wanted each and every one of our employees to know how vital and important they were to our organization. I wanted the people who were cleaning and servicing our cars to know that we were there for them, that we believed in them, and that we were all in it together. I wanted each of them to know that they can truly make a difference—in the lives of our clients, our company, and each other.

So, I pulled my senior leadership team together and said, "We are on a new mission, with a new vision, and a new team. We need to set a new tone, and to get our message out there." I quickly added that this was not in any way, shape, or form to take away from the past. Then I wondered out loud, "How can we connect with our people, to help them see that we are in it together, and that we mean what we are saying?"

"Prior to Tom becoming president," explained Ned Linnen, who is now the executive vice president and chief human resources officer at Avis Budget Group, "for us to communicate with our employees, we would generally create posters and put them up in our break rooms, since only a small percentage of our employees had access to computers. We were a break-room culture. That was how we described ourselves. So, someone on the executive team said to Tom, 'We could create a really creative poster.' Someone else said, 'We could create a dynamic email campaign.' And Tom just sat there, shaking his head back and forth."

DO SOMETHING THAT IS FRIGGIN' CRAZY

As we explored options, I just started to smile. Then I said, "I got it. Let's get a bus and travel to each of our locations around the country."

Ned recalled that he just thought I was kidding. Then when he realized I was serious, he said he could not help himself. He just blurted out, "You're friggin' crazy."

I laughed so hard when he said that. I thought his comment was hysterical, in the moment, and real. And I also loved that he felt comfortable saying it out loud to me.

The executive team went on to cite reason after reason for why my idea, while inspiring, was completely impractical. It was not just daunting, they emphasized. It was overwhelming to even consider the magnitude of the challenge. Avis's twenty thousand employees were spread over five thousand locations. The executives reminded me that we had enormous challenges facing us as a leadership team, and our calendars were full of meetings we needed to attend. As they continued to talk about how many months it would take for us to visit each of our locations, I realized I was on to something.

My idea, as I enthusiastically shared with the team, was to get a bus and have it reconfigured into offices and wired with Wi-Fi, so we could work as we traveled between locations. Then we would go to each location and personally thank every one of our employees for what they were doing. We would share success stories. And we would convey our vision for the future—and how we were all going to succeed together.

That is how we started to change the culture of the organization. By trying something that was "friggin' crazy."

We devised a systematic logistics path through North America that allowed us to hug, shake hands with, look into the eyes of, and personally thank 80 percent of the people who were part of our organization. We identified a hundred airport locations where we could see most of our employees. To have the broadest reach, we went to off-airport local markets and transported as many of our employees as we could—so that the connections we were creating became ubiquitous.

Our commitment was passionate and unwavering. We would start out Sunday night and spend the entire week traveling, sometimes visiting three locations a day, where we would hold a rally that lasted at least four hours. That is how we covered 22,000 miles over the course of eleven weeks, all the while creating powerful connections.

I insisted that none of us would get on stage to speak before we shook everybody's hands and looked them in the eye and said, "Thank you." I said, "We want everyone to get out of bed in the morning feeling really good about what they are doing."

There were four of us in it together, sharing every leg of the journey. In addition to Ned, there was Gina Bruzzichesi, our senior vice president of strategic customer leadership; Joe Ferraro, our senior vice president of North American operations; and me. Over time, we refined our messages and made them very crisp. But the point was that we were all in it together and tied at the hip. Our goal was to share our new vision—which was that each and every one of us could have a significant impact on our success. *I Own It* became our motto. But the "I" was never alone because we believed in *Family First*. Not just because we are a work family, but because we also cared about each other's families at home.

Then I would emphasize that we were all there to *Do the Right Thing*. That we had integrity. And, finally, I would underscore that we were all in it to *Win* (to instill a sense of competitiveness).

I would share stories from every place we stopped about how someone in that location had emphasized those four core values. Then Joe would connect the dots, explaining to everyone how individuals who had gone the extra mile were helping in very big ways to make our company—and all of us—profitable. Gina would then share stories about the experiences we were creating for our customers, and how we could significantly improve our scores with J.D. Power. And Ned would close with a message about the importance of taking care of your health, as well as how many of our people were able to send their children to college for the first time, and how we were touching each other's lives.

We received encouraging feedback that the stories each of us told on that tour resonated with our people. Just by way of a quick example, Ned told a story about how, when he was younger, he thought he would live forever, so, as he said, "I was a little crazy and didn't take care of myself at all. I didn't really care how much I ate, drank, exercised, or slept. Then one night, it was around two o'clock in the morning, I ended up in an emergency room. It was St. Patrick's Day. And I realized I had to do something different about my health. I wasn't thinking about myself, but about the birth of our first son. I realized that I could have missed everything afterward. That was my motivation. I wanted to live longer for him."

So that next morning, as Ned told the group, he started running. "Three years later," he said, "I had my daughter. And I started running more. And I would say to everyone, 'Find something positive in your life to be your motivation to make you change. If you wait until the next tragedy to be your motivation, it may be too late. Take care of yourself—for those you love."

Two years after that tour, Ned was in Tulsa, and a woman came up to him and said, "I'm sure you don't recognize me."

Feeling embarrassed, as we often do when we do not recognize someone, he said, "I'm sorry, I don't."

She replied, "The reason you don't recognize me is because I lost 112 pounds." Then she explained, "I lost all of that weight because of you. I listened to your speech. And you said to find your motivation. And you said not to let your next tragedy be your motivation." She added, "I remembered that. And I lost a lot of weight. And my husband lost 123 pounds. And I just want to thank you."

Ned said, "I never would have opened myself up like that if it wasn't for Tom. I would not have ever thought about making that speech."

The message we were conveying to everyone was: *We cannot win by ourselves. Everybody owns it. And we all need each other.* It does not matter where you are from; what matters is where we are going together. With those core ideas in mind, we communicated to everyone the importance of thinking and acting like a work family, treating everyone with respect and dignity.

CUSTOMER EXPERIENCE OWNERS

Looking back on the journey, Gina, who was in her last trimester with her first child on our tour, smiled and said, "I was very much pregnant, and my daughter Emersyn was born the day after we ended the tour. It was like she was there with us all the way. I was forty-one at the time, having my baby as I always wanted. And doing it on tour with the rest of the senior leadership team. We embraced my pregnancy on the tour and celebrated it. I was spending time with my work family, and being real."

Gina spoke about the CEO experience, "which was about all of us—because we are all 'Customer Experience Owners.'" She encouraged everyone to see that any of our customers who looked distressed became perfect opportunities for us to turn that situation around and create memorable experiences for them that would make their days.

Then she would highlight people in each location who had recently come through for our customers with flying colors. All of us would then rally around and celebrate each of these individuals who represented us at our best. We asked them to share stories about how they connected with a customer who was complaining, and how they turned that person around into an advocate and believer in who we were. There was a palpable excitement as stories were told about our team members who created memorable experiences for our customers. The message was clear: *It was our people who set us apart. If it were not for them, we would be just another commodity.* Instead, they were creating lasting impressions for our customers—and we were letting them know how very much they meant to all of us.

As we went from city to city, I felt a natural connection to—and wanted to be with—our people who were working on the lines day in and day out. Part of my bond with them came from having worked in a steel fabricating plant early in my career. So, I felt a natural connection to—and wanted to be with—our people who were working directly with our customers.

And when we met, the connection was deeper, more uplifting and fulfilling, than I could have possibly imagined or hoped for. Hearts were opened as we shared laughter, tears, and stories about being there for each other and coming through for our customers.

In fact, I often got so emotionally involved in what I was learning about their unwavering dedication and commitment that I would just start tearing up. More often than not, when I was speaking, tears would start to form and my voice would crack because I truly cared so much about the people I was meeting. Their personal stories affected me deeply. I could not help it. Sharing their stories connected us in ways we never could have imagined—and made clear how we would all succeed together. And our hugs spoke louder than words.

The last day of the tour, as we were heading back to our corporate office, I thought, "I don't know if people back at headquarters will understand what happened." There was so much excitement and energy every place we stopped. Then it hit me, and I said to my team, "Let's pull together the people who told the most inspirational stories, the ones who epitomize our work together, and bring them to headquarters with us, and let them tell their stories."

And that presentation was inspiring.

There was a man from Chicago who had worked forty-five years and never missed a day of work. There was a man in Kansas City who worked three consecutive days around the clock because we were short-staffed. And there was a woman from Detroit who had more customer compliments than anyone else in our history. When we brought them all back to headquarters, and everyone listened to them tell their stories, you could hear a pin drop.

And everyone got it—because we were all experiencing it together. We were starting to think about our company as a family. As Ned Linnen recalled, "There was a feeling and sentiment that was the beginning of a cultural change."

I understood that you cannot change culture through emails. As a leader, you cannot truly connect by staying in your ivory tower. The only way to connect is in person. And you can only do that one person at a time.

I knew that getting out and connecting with everyone was vitally important. In fact, I felt that it could be the lynchpin for the future success of our business. It was as simple as getting out there with everyone, rolling up our sleeves, and saying, "How's it going? What's working? What can we improve? How are you doing?"

Sure, I understood that we were in a commodity business. People go to an airport, and they have the choice of renting a car from many different vendors. So, of course, I understood the importance of managing costs and price to show a profit. That is always important in any business.

But that alone was not going to create our differentiator.

CREATING DEEP CONNECTIONS

Demonstrating that we cared for each other, and that we were all in it together—that would start to change our culture. It was a matter of tapping into a feeling that I knew was already there in the people around me.

We were starting to think about the company as a family. That sentiment started to come through like never before.

Late that summer, New Orleans was hit by Hurricane Isaac. And we were all stunned by the devastation. It was hard to get information about our employees, many of whom we had just been celebrating with in early June. Where were they? How were they? Had anyone lost their homes? Their loved ones? Amid the chaos and uncertainty, our managers in the city started going to these centers where people were gathering. And they found our employees and took them to hotels that we had booked.

Of course, all the rental companies were closed. That was the last thing on our minds. But, somehow, 90 percent of our employees showed up to work the next day, which was the last thing I expected. They did not need to. Some of their houses were flooded. Everyone in our company was aware of the devastation and asking about how each of our employees was doing.

The next day, I called Ned and said, "I already talked to Ron and I have his approval to use the corporate jet." I told him, "Our people in New Orleans have not had a hot meal for days. So, I want to go down there with our leadership team." I told him that I had spoken to a guy who could get us two gas grills. We were going to fill the plane up with all the food we could grill. Then I added, "This is just a small way for us to do the right thing."

I asked Ned if he would check with his wife, Ann Marie, and make sure she was fine with this. And Ned said, "I already did." Incredulous, I asked, "How could you have?" And he said, "Because I knew you would be calling. So, I already asked her."

So, Ron Nelson, Joe Ferraro, Ned, and I flew down on Labor Day Monday and gathered together with our employees, whom we had just seen a few months before on The Bus Tour. There was a woman at the counter whom I recognized. I asked her, "How are you doing?" She just started crying. And I said, "You *would* do this for us, wouldn't you?"

She replied, "I would now."

It was a truly impactful moment. It was the point where a personal connection deepened.

Then Hurricane Sandy hit, and our people in New Orleans immediately started raising money for the people in New Jersey.

We were all feeling the depth of our connection. It came from reaching out to each other. We had created real and lasting connections based on our hearts, which transcended boundaries and created new possibilities for all of us.

REMIND EVERYONE OF WHO THEY ARE—AT THEIR BEST

The first year we did The Bus Tour, we also trained every manager on how to be a leader. The three executives on the bus and I delivered the training. Of course, most companies will hire trainers to do that. But this was a personal commitment for us. We trained each level of management to enhance their personal and leadership skills. We brought them all into our headquarters. My belief was that *you can train all you want, but if it does not come from the heart, it will not connect.*

Ultimately, we wanted every one of our managers to know that we believed in them as leaders, and that we were looking for them to shepherd the careers of the people around them. During the course of that year, we moved about seventy-five people into new roles. So, the impact was real. I recall in one of the sessions we did in Dallas, I got up on stage and said, "Whoever is in a new role this year, please stand up." And nearly half of the room stood. We were moving people who were really smart into new roles. And they loved it.

At the end of that year, our employee engagement scores went through the roof. In fact, the research scientist from Gelfond, who did the survey, said, "We think there is something wrong with your results."

I asked, "Why?"

He replied, "Because we have never seen results move like this in thirty years."

I just said, "I think they are probably true."

And he responded, "No. They can't be."

So, I said, "Let me tell you what happened this year."

As I told him about everything I just shared with you, he said, "Okay. So that makes sense. But you are screwed next year!"

I just shook my head and said, "Geez. Why do you say that?"

"Because if you don't do those same things over, and over, and over again, your score is going to go down."

I just smiled, and said, "That will be easy. We will not only do those same things over; we'll add some new things." The people we have working for us are incredible. They get up in the middle of the night. And they travel to work through rain and snowstorms. We just need to find a way to thank them and let them know how much we care. And to make sure that they feel good about getting out of bed to go to work every day.

As a result of all we were doing together, the first year our employee engagement scores went up eleven points. We were ecstatic, because the rise was historic. Then the second year, after being warned that it would difficult to even maintain that level of initial enthusiasm, we defied the odds, and went up six more points. And then the next year, our scores went up four more points on top of that. It was three consecutive years of going up. It was fun and amazing—together, we were building an engaged work family, who cared about and were coming through for our customers and each other.

Bob Chaps, who was a regional sales vice president at that time, shared an interesting perspective on what else might have been influencing the way I was thinking and feeling. He said, "When Tom came to our company, it was his 'outsider's view' that allowed him to see what was great in our company. He recognized, brought out, and harnessed the energy of our company in a way that really moved us forward—and took advantage of what was always there and what was our essence—which we had either taken for granted or not been able to recognize. He saw us all with fresh eyes. It was something the rest of us who had been there forever were missing. His outsider's view helped us see ourselves better."

What I did was remind them of who they were—at their best. And everyone responded by saying, "Yeah! That's who we are."

It just took me reminding everyone that we are all part of a larger family. Then I helped them recognize that we are all in it together. And I celebrated them.

Let me conclude this chapter with something that Ned said: "I'm not a typical human resources guy. Because I'm not very emotional. So, Tom and I made an interesting pair. I remember one time on the tour when Tom was talking about his daughter, who was very sick. And he broke down and started crying. And I thought, that was a large part of what the tour conveyed. It was our saying that we can be leaders of this company and be just as real and honest and vulnerable as you. And that is what Tom is all about. He helped all of us become more real, more relatable."

Ned laughed, then added, "I continually tell Tom that it makes me uncomfortable when he cries. Then he'll give me a big hug, and I'll say, 'That makes me uncomfortable, too.' But you know what I like about it? He is who he is. And he has a way of showing everybody else that it is okay to be who you are."

One of the most important lessons I have learned as a leader is that by blurring the lines between what is traditionally thought of as "professional" and "personal," and by truly caring about those with whom you are working, you will inspire them to commit themselves, and come through for you, in ways that will absolutely astound you. And they will help to make you an even better leader as a result.

WHAT DOES YOUR ORGANIZATION VALUE? (HINT: IT HAS A LOT TO DO WITH WHAT YOU MEASURE AND REWARD.)

Your values describe who you are. And who you are not. They reflect your understanding of what is right. And what is wrong. They become your inner compass, your reference point for how you will act. When you make a decision, your values clarify what is not negotiable. They are your declaration of what you stand for. And what you will not stand for.

As a leader, you want your values to be clear as a bell. And you want that bell to ring loudly. And often.

To put their faith in you as a leader, people first want to know who you are. Then, with that solid understanding and belief in you, they will sign up for your journey together.

Ultimately, people want to know that they are part of something that they can believe in, that is meaningful, and where they can make a difference. And they want to know that you have the principles and backbone to lead them on the right path to places they never even imagined.

Your leadership journey all starts with the values you believe in and bring alive—within yourself and inside your organization.

On this journey, we recognized our guiding principles as:

- being there for and truly caring for each other *(Family First)*,

- being committed *(Working Half-Days)*,
- creating memorable experiences for our customers *(Do the Right Thing)*,
- being true to each other *(Words Plus Actions Matching)*,
- knowing that each of us could make a difference *(I Own It)*, and
- succeeding together *(Winning)*.

What are your key values? And how do your express them?

Here is a partial list of values. I encourage you to review them. Add any you feel may be missing. Then circle the three that are at the heart of who you are. Which ones are you at your very best? Which values are at the core of your being?

Accountability	Financial Stability
Achievement	Flexibility
Adaptability	Fun
Authenticity	Happiness
Balance (Home/Work)	Helping Others
Bravery	Honesty
Compassion	Honor
Creativity	Hope
Curiosity	Integrity
Engagement	Initiative
Fairness	Love
Family	Loyalty

Making a Difference   Risk-Taking
Meaningful Work   Self-Discipline
Open Communication   Social Intelligence
Open-Mindedness   Teamwork
Optimism   Trust
Patience   Uniqueness
Professional Growth   Vision
Realizing Potential   Vulnerability
Relationships   Well-Being
Respect   Wisdom
Responsibility   Other: _____

Are you most interested in accountability or authenticity? Are you more about bravery or compassion? Do you look for creativity or fairness? How important is caring and having fun to you? Are you looking for initiative or loyalty? Do you want to make a difference and have meaningful work? Are you seeking financial stability or unprecedented growth? Are you most interested in open communication or optimism? Are you about potential, respect, responsibility, or risk-taking? Do you value trust and teamwork? Or is there another value that is at your core?

Which three values speak to you most? Which ones call out to you? Which ones do you embody? Which ones, for you, are non-negotiable?

Just consider how you might be thinking and feeling about yourself—and others—if you are wearing those three values on your sleeve.

Imagine yourself turning up the volume on how you express your values. How would you be leading differently if you were clearer about your values?

At the end of the day, you can tell a lot about a leader—and the organization he or she is leading—by the values that they share out loud. The easiest way to tell what an organization values is to see what it measures. What are you recognizing and rewarding? The answer to that question also answers the ultimate question: *What do you really believe in?*

SOMETIMES IT TAKES BEING FRIGGIN' CRAZY: QUESTIONS FOR SELF-EVALUATION

The questions we ask ourselves, and how deeply we answer them, help to shape who we become. With that in mind, I encourage you to dive deeply as you explore these questions. Then review your answers from time to time. And allow your answers to evolve. Your answers will serve as road signs on your leadership journey.

1. So, what will be your Bus Tour? How will you connect more deeply with everyone in your organization?
2. What is your organization's most important strength?
3. How can you make that strength even more prominent, visible, and empowering?
4. What do you most want to change about the culture of your organization? Do you believe you can change that?
5. What major step can you take to make that change?
6. What is the next thing you would change?
7. Are you fully committed? (How much time and effort are you willing to put into making your culture vibrant?)
8. Are you able to persuade those in your organization who are not as committed as you to go along for the journey?

CHAPTER 6

RECOGNIZING THE POTENTIAL IN PEOPLE

When you lead with your heart, you believe in people. You get close with them, connect with their hearts, and, in the process, see something that often they do not even recognize—their potential. Then you nourish that potential, and you grow together.

As a leader, I believe that identifying potential and developing talent are *the most important contributions you can make to your organization.* This has become one of my main focuses. It is the ability to recognize, value, reward, appreciate, and personally let people know how vital they are. In fact, I believe one of my most notable accomplishments as a leader was recognizing the potential of several individuals who could have been easily overlooked—and, instead, went on to become high-performing leaders.

SEEING NEW POSSIBILITIES IN OTHERS

In all honesty, it took some time for me to develop this way of looking at those around me. It is not uncommon, and undoubtedly natural, for those of us who want to be seen as leaders to draw attention to ourselves early in our careers. We want to stand out from the crowd. We are seeking to be noticed for our unique qualities. We are looking for recognition of our accomplishments. We are raising our hands and asking to be seen.

That is why our leadership potential has to marinate. It takes time for the realization to sink in that leading is not about us. It is about others. We need to see beyond ourselves. In addition to having a vision, and being able to inspire others, growing as a leader is about recognizing the potential in those around you. It is about being able to recognize the kernel inside of people that is yearning to be seen. I knew that this transformation from "me" to "we," from focusing on myself to seeing the importance in others, had finally transpired for me when I was able to walk into a room saying, "Hey, look at you!" instead of thinking, "Hey, look at me."

Seeing the potential in people takes time, a shift in focus, practice, and care. It takes getting close to those around you. And learning what is in their hearts and minds. What are their dreams and fears, their doubts and hopes, their troubles and aspirations?

This is not just something that you do every now and then. It is a skill you can develop. But first, you need to recognize that *leading is not about you right now. Leading is about seeing the future in others.*

When I arrived at Avis, I set the stage for who I was and what I wanted to accomplish. With a very strategic, focused approach, I brought a Talent Management Process to the sales organization. I said to everyone in management that we were going to spend several days going over our top-talent, high-potential performers, those in the middle, and anyone about whom we had any concerns. And I promised we would do this annually.

Bob Chaps, who was a regional sales vice president at that time, recalled, "We were all a little skeptical. Prior to that, we would have a spreadsheet about our people, which we would update yearly, then put it in a file. So, we thought, 'Is this process actionable and sustainable?'"

I began by collaborating with Barbara Kogen, who was the vice president of organizational development and performance, to develop a way to assess the competencies that were needed to excel in sales within our organization. "Tom was a key driver in getting consistent competencies across the sales organization," Barbara said. "For instance, he wanted to make sure that everyone in sales management had 'managerial courage.' By that, he meant that he was looking for managers who would be open and direct with others, as they tactfully provided honest feedback, while also being clear about the required outcomes. So, he unmistakably set the stage for what would be expected."

Barbara and her team then created a consistent process and a method for our managers to assess our sales talent.

Barbara explained, "Essentially, we were looking at the performance and potential of individuals. What had they accomplished? And what did we believe they were capable of?" She added, "What Tom brought was a discipline and commitment to make the process consistent and rigorous across the entire sales organization."

Among my key questions were: Who are our high-potential employees? Are we recognizing and rewarding them? Are we letting them know how important they are to us? And what are we doing to make sure that our top performers have a career plan that aligns their aspirations with the organization's goals?

Keep in mind that I was introducing this assessment process in the beginning of 2009, as the economy was starting to fall apart at the seams. So, during that time, while parts of our appraisals were subjective and others objective, the major question we were asking was: If we have a huge workforce reduction coming, who would we keep, no matter what? Such individuals were high-potential. If we had to eliminate the jobs of such individuals, we would keep them and move them to another area because they were *that* important to us. During those tenuous times, that question became a marker for someone who was high-potential.

With that in mind, I pulled the entire sales management team together, and I explained that I wanted each of them to share insights into the people reporting to them. Then I was going to ask everybody at the table what they were thinking and feeling—not just the person who was the manager. And we would each do this, one at a time. I encouraged everyone to talk about each person on their team in a holistic way. I would ask, "Is there a more appropriate role in our organization for this person? Could he or she help us succeed better somewhere else?" Then I shared what I was hearing, thinking, and feeling. And I made detailed notes to myself as I listened carefully to what our leaders were saying about the people with whom they worked.

Barbara added, "Tom also set the tone that when we did employee performance reviews, everyone in the room was sworn to an oath of confidentiality. He was clear that if anything leaked from the room concerning what we were saying about an employee, whoever leaked it would be gone. Period. End of sentence. In order to establish trust, Tom underscored, that trust could not be broken. He was definite about that. And he never did it by raising his voice. He just expressed it with a firmness and conviction. And everyone understood it."

To make this process meaningful, I knew we needed to create an environment where managers felt they had the right to talk about the performance of people in ways that were open and honest. This could only be done among managers who felt that everything they expressed about the people they were working with was said in complete confidence. For this approach to work, I knew that we needed to have faith in one another, so I set the ground rules. *Trust needed to be built from the ground up.*

We were all talking about the talent and potential of the people with whom we surrounded ourselves. I needed our conversations to be frank and open. So, confidentiality, trust, and candor were necessary. We were going to do what was right for people and for the organization.

Bob said, "These were not the kind of conversations we had ever had before. Tom wanted to know who had ability and passion, and who did not. Then after the meeting, there were actions taken. One person got a warning. Another person got promoted. Someone else was moved to a whole different division. There were actions that happened immediately after that meeting. And all of us looked up and around, and said, 'This is different.'"

I was delivering two messages in that meeting. One was that I felt it was vitally important for all of us together to spend two days dedicated to focusing on the talent in our organization. The other message was that we were going to make decisions and act on them together—with their buy-in, based on what they said and believed.

In addition, if someone was identified as a high-potential employee, after the meeting, I arranged to spend two days with them in their environment. (This approach comes from my early days in field sales management.) I knew that high-potential individuals thrive on receiving that kind of attention from leadership. And, equally important, it allowed me an opportunity to glean a unique view into each individual's character. Being with someone for an hour or two can give you a glimpse into some of the qualities and values inside them. But spending two days with someone gives you a much deeper, clearer, and more consistent understanding of how they think, feel, and behave under a variety of circumstances.

How you handle this process gives people who are interested in moving up in the organization the confidence to give it their all—and lets them know that they can be rewarded for high-level performance.

When I was with our high-potential people, I would counsel them on their career development by saying, "Take what you are best at, what you love to do, and develop that to its fullest. As you are doing that, look inside our organization and see how you can take your potential and your talent as far as you possibly can."

Our talent is what distinguishes us, I underscored constantly, in every way I knew how. And that talent will grow in ways that we cannot even imagine—if we continually pay attention to the potential and aspirations of those who are our future.

Whenever I am with someone in our organization or with someone who I am considering bringing into our organization, I am always looking for the same thing: their potential. Of course, I am interested in what they have accomplished. But I am less focused on what has been than on what can be.

FACTORS TO CONSIDER

A large part of someone's growth potential has to do with how comfortable he or she is with change—inside themselves and within the company. Regardless of how talented an individual may be, does he or she view change as exciting or concerning? For those with high potential, the future, while unknown, is full of possibilities. As you look to grow your organization, and to create a culture focused on potential, you want to surround yourself with talented individuals who are enthused about new possibilities—for themselves and for your organization.

Ultimately, leadership is about understanding the strengths and aspirations of the individuals you surround yourself with—and then strategically aligning those individuals with the future needs of your organization.

Seeing the potential in others is a unique ability to gaze into the future. Part of it has to do with seeing what is. Most of it has to do with perceiving what can be. Often it is something intangible that you sense in someone else. Sometimes what you sense is very specific, such as a drive to achieve, or an uncanny ability to connect with others, or an astonishing capacity for recovering from setbacks and carrying on with even more determination. Whenever I sense a certain potential in someone else, for me, that realization also comes with a certain responsibility. I feel it is my obligation to help that individual's potential see the light of day. It is as if I am helping to create the future—for that individual, and for our organization. And when that individual realizes his or her potential, I feel an enormous sense of awe and gratitude.

Sometimes just by seeing the potential in someone else, you can help them to bring those possibilities alive in themselves. Sometimes you may be seeing potential in someone that they do not see.

And sometimes you see potential in someone, but others disagree with you. I recall being particularly surprised when Ron Nelson, our chairman, challenged me about one of our senior leaders who was reporting to me. She was, I assured him, a true talent, with enormous capability. I then asked him if he would take two days and work with her to experience how she was as a leader with her team and what she was like in front of our clients.

I was keenly aware that asking for two days of our chairman's time was a huge request. Still, he agreed, without hesitating. And that told me two very important things about him. First, while Ron is a leader with a clear and strong viewpoint, he is also open to considering that there might be a better way to move forward. And second, as I mentioned before, I realized that I was personally in a very enviable position as a leader—because Ron let me know that I had his trust and support, and I am very grateful to him for that. With his belief in me, I was able to lead in a way that was allowing me to transform our business through personal connections.

So, with Ron's consent, the meetings were scheduled, six weeks out, for him to travel for two days with our senior leader whose potential we each saw differently. I did not tell her that this was a test, that she was being challenged. Instead, I just allowed her to feel that this was an opportunity for her to shine with our chairman in front of some of our key clients. I wanted her to feel completely positive and confident in this situation. And I intuitively felt that this was the perfect situation for her to shine. I knew she had the potential. The opportunity to demonstrate that potential is what I was seeking for her. I also knew that since she was much more confident in front of her clients, this was an ideal setting for our chairman to see her at her very best.

When they both returned from their two days on the road together, I could tell things had gone exceedingly well. Ron told me that his feelings toward her had changed completely. And, I have no doubt, that the change in his feeling toward her was reflected in her showing up even more confidently. All I had done was to politely challenge our chairman's assumptions, create an opportunity for her, then work with her as part of our ongoing coaching. And this changed the trajectory of her career, as she is now a global leader in the organization.

CREATING OPENINGS FOR NEW POSSIBILITIES

Another individual whose potential I immediately recognized was Stephen Wright, who was vice president of sales for Canada when I worked with him. I understood that he had the potential to work up and down an organization and connect the dots with people and ideas. However, he needed a larger arena to share his talents. In our organization, Canada did not offer the opportunities for his talents to thrive. I knew that if we could move him into our corporate arena, where he could work on a bigger stage, and if I could work closely with him, he could open up to new possibilities.

But I also knew he was reluctant to uproot his family from the place they felt was home. I understood that completely, since I have such strong roots in St. Paul.

So, rather than coax Stephen to take a promotion at headquarters right away and relocate his family to a new country, I spent time coaching him, deepening our personal connection, and developing a greater level of trust with him.

At first, I helped him, as Stephen said, "to understand the importance and depth of relationships at a whole new level." As a result, he was becoming much more effective at sales. I knew that he understood how to work on Elevation Plans, which is having your professional relationships help you to get to the highest level you can within an organization. So, I introduced him to the Cell Approach, which, in essence, is developing such deep relationships with your clients that they are willing to introduce you to *their* clients and colleagues.

Stephen flourished by embracing this concept. He had a very close relationship with the CEO of Air Canada. So, Stephen asked this executive if he had any colleagues in other companies whom he felt might benefit from the services of Avis Budget Group. The Air Canada executive introduced Stephen to the chief executive officer of Air Asia, who eventually became a very valuable client.

It is all about realizing the importance of relationships, then drilling down deep. Stephen added, "Focusing more on the relationship and allowing everything else to follow is a powerful lesson that I learned from Tom."

Rather than thinking about the next sale, I was coaching Stephen to focus more on the relationships he had, and to believe that, because of that attention, other doors would open.

After Stephen and I had worked closely together and developed a deep level of trust, and he believed that I had taken a personal interest in him and his career, I knew the time had arrived to ask him to consider moving to New Jersey, where Avis Budget Group's headquarters is, to take on the role of vice president of key accounts for North America. He knew I believed in him—and would be there for him and his family.

At first, Stephen tried to convince me that he could do the job from Toronto. But I insisted. "You need to be at headquarters. You need face time with the other leaders here. If you are not here," I told him, "you will be perceived as someone who is not interested in advancing your career."

As Stephen explained, "I went home and spent a lot of time talking it over with my wife. Then I also spent quite a bit of time talking with Tom about it. Then I said, 'I'm in.' And Tom was absolutely right. The exposure I got certainly helped to accelerate my career."

Stephen added, "That is where Tom came through in spades. He took a very personal interest in my career development—as well as in me and my family. Don't get me wrong. I was held accountable. It was no cakewalk. But he really came through in making me and my family feel welcomed and a part of his family. He overdelivered on his promises. That's what he did and who he is. When we came down, he had a party for us. We met with his wife, Barb, and his family. We were at his house in Minnesota, then saw a hockey game with him and his family. We felt very welcomed into his family. We have seen plays with him in New York, gone to dinner with him. It really is one big family because of him." He paused, then added, "He's not in the organization today, but my wife still sends him an email every couple of weeks."

Stephen continued, "He makes you want to work hard for him. By showing his caring and his love, you want to help him succeed. And in order for him to be successful, we all have to be successful. So, you work your tail off to make sure he is successful. It is leadership at its best. When you care for people, they will do anything for you. It's the recognition and the collaboration. It is recognizing what everyone brings to the table. I believe that is what he is all about. With Tom, it is always a 'we.' It is never a 'me' or an 'I.' He blends the personal with the professional more than anyone I've ever met before. But you also have to perform. There was a clear sense of accountability. I knew if there was ever a time that I was not performing, I would be held accountable. No question."

He concluded, "The love he shows is more than I have ever seen or experienced from a leader ever before in my life."

People who are interested in moving up in an organization want to know that there is a path for them to be recognized and rewarded. As a leader, you need to identify such individuals, groom them, and create a path for them. This opens up several questions you will want to explore, including: How can you help a promising individual to see and develop the talent within themselves? Are you aware of the aspirations of your high-potential and top-performing people? And, equally important, can you identify the future needs for your organization—in a world that is ever changing?

A large part of sensing someone else's potential also has to do with following your intuition. It takes believing in yourself—and in the person whose potential you are sensing.

UNDERSTAND SOMEONE FIRST

You also have to take a risk on people that you believe in. I am a relationship guy first and foremost. For me, it is personal. My comfort zone is to understand someone first, then seek to help them find their career trajectory in the company.

For instance, I knew that Gina Bruzzichesi, who was the customer experience leader when we undertook The Bus Tour, aspired to head up an organization. She started with the company as an attorney. I connected with her because of her very positive approach, passion, and attitude. Early on, she gained experience by being in the field, living the life of the people who make the organization tick. She was willing to take on any new challenge to expand her experience and to help the organization. When we brought Payless Car Rental into the organization, we needed a leader to integrate that brand. Even though Gina had not been an operational leader before, I knew, from working with her closely, that she could rise to the challenge.

What seemed to surprise many people was that I also chose to promote her to senior vice president of Payless when she was pregnant, but that did not concern me in the least. Having worked with Gina on The Bus Tour when she was pregnant her first time, I knew that I was going to have to coach her to slow down from time to time, and make sure that she was taking care of herself personally. That was my only concern. Because I knew that Gina, like most over-achievers, would continually push herself to make sure she succeeded.

"To promote a pregnant woman into a high-profile, high-stress leadership position in which the company was looking for a big return was a huge leap of faith. That was a risk," Gina said. "But Tom took that chance on me, and, with his guidance, I was able to thrive in that role. I was able to spend more time with him—focusing on marketing, sales, and revenue generation, which, of course, are his areas of expertise."

Together, we spent time together focusing on aspects of running the business that were new to her, including operations and revenue generation. We also strategized and talked long and hard about how to integrate Payless into our organization. "Tom enabled me, guided me, and taught me an enormous amount through that experience," Gina added. "I learned how to manage both sides of the P&L—from sales to operations. Then we spent a lot of time strategizing about the branding, the customer values and messaging, how to introduce Payless to different channels, and how to keep the brand distinct, while incorporating it into our organization."

Ultimately, we decided to integrate the new brand slowly because we needed to understand what made Payless tick. While optimizing efficiencies, we also wanted to make sure that we did not lose the positive attributes of Payless by making it too much like the rest of our organization. I encouraged Gina to take some time understanding that important nuance and to resist the natural reaction of most people in the organization who wanted everything to happen quickly. "Tom coached me on how to take a long-term view toward success, while keeping an even keel, and standing my ground, as I worked with others through the twists and turns to get where I eventually wanted to go." She paused, then added, "Most importantly, what I learned from Tom, almost through osmosis, is how to connect with people on a deeper level. At times, it is about being patient and listening, creating a sense of caring and collaboration. At other times, it is about knowing when to put your foot on the accelerator and forge ahead."

SEEING AN OPPORTUNITY AND RAISING YOUR HAND

My goal was for everyone to look at each other more positively and the organization more holistically. It is not uncommon for people within organizations to exist in separate, self-contained silos, organized by department—sales in its own arena, operations off on its own, finance autonomous, and so forth. But I could see the connections, and I wanted to strengthen them. I was most interested in looking

beyond those silos, seeing how people could grow in different areas of the company. I was thinking about everyone's
talent, potential, and aspirations.

*I was developing a culture where people felt comfortable
raising their hands and asking to be considered for a new
opportunity.* I wanted to encourage people to step up and
take ownership of their careers. I have always liked people
who raise their hands and ask if they can move into a new
situation. Such individuals clearly are self-confident and
comfortable getting outside of their own comfort zone.

There are others who prefer to stay in their lane: do their
job well, then go home and leave work behind. I understand
that. But I am much more interested in those who have
gumption. Those are the ones who see an opportunity and
raise their hand and ask if they can step in. I have always
been drawn to those who have a sense of determination,
enthusiasm, and pluck. They make things happen. At the
end of the day—if we learned nothing else from school—if
we don't raise our hands, we won't get called on.

One individual who raised his hand was Tom Villani,
who was a pricing manager before I eventually promoted
him to vice president, global travel and partnerships.

When I first became president, I took the pricing department out to breakfast. I saw those in the department as vital
to our success. Looking back at himself as a young pricing
manager, Tom Villani said, "In that first meeting, [Tom]
described his vision and goals, and we were all stunned that
he would even pay attention to us. Then he got to know all
of us on the pricing committee, which had never been done

before. We were never recognized. Ever. Then he started taking us out to dinner once a quarter, and giving us bonuses for helping to hit specific goals. He knew us by name. He got to know us personally. And we learned that once he said he was going to do something, he did it. And that really mattered. So, we believed in this man. He showed us how important we were to the organization. And in turn, we were willing to climb any mountain or go through any fire for him."

It sounds simple, and like most truths, it is: *treat people well and it will come back to you in spades.*

I immediately saw this young man as someone who could be a driver of business for our company. Together we worked on major deals with several Fortune 500 companies that had a huge impact on our organization.

As our relationship grew, what was professional and personal blended. It was not unusual for Barb and me to go out for dinner with Tom and his wife, Dotti, on a Friday night. We always went to the same place, Café Navona. Tom Villani recalled how one night he and his wife went to Navona by themselves. "The owner came by and said, 'Are your parents coming tonight?' And I said to my wife, 'They think we're Tom's kids.'"

We had a good laugh over that. Afterward, I could not help but smile, as I thought about what a unique compliment it was to have the waitstaff at Navona recognize the personal connection between Tom, Dotti, Barb, and me—and to assume that it meant we were "family."

I cannot emphasize enough that although so many corporate leaders find the need to distance themselves from those they are leading, this does not make an ounce of sense to me. As my career progressed, getting closer to those whom I respect and admire has enriched my life personally and professionally. And I am forever grateful.

It is important to add, as Tom Villani said about my expectations back then, "As a leader, he always set very high standards. And you had to meet them. There was nothing confusing about that. He was not going to take it easy on me because we were friends. Quite the opposite. I believe that because we were (and are) friends, he may have expected a little bit more of me, just as I expected a little bit more of myself. And through it all, we had such a strong connection that I would never let him down. Just as I would never let any friend down."

OVERCOME THE NATURAL TENDENCY TO "TYPECAST" PEOPLE

Are you open to thinking about someone's potential? Can you see them in a new light? Do you know what drives them—and where that drive can take them?

When I make personal connections with people I work with, I am always interested in seeing their potential, then helping them to thrive. Keep in mind, however, that someone's potential may have absolutely nothing to do with what they have previously accomplished. In fact, what they have done might actually get in the way of your seeing their potential.

To see someone's potential, we have to overcome a natural tendency to "typecast" people. We have all heard actors in Hollywood bemoan being repeatedly assigned to the same type of roles because of their appearance or previous success in such roles. As leaders, we need to be aware of typecasting, whether we are considering a promotion for someone within our organization or looking to hire in someone new. Typecasting can become an easy, yet short-sighted and misguided, way of considering someone's previous experience.

Many leaders prefer to look to their competitors' backyards when they are hiring. They consider that experience to be valuable. If two candidates seem equally qualified and one has more "experience" in the industry, the decision seems easy. Experience wins. Perhaps the experienced candidate will even bring some clients along. At the very least, they will hit the ground running. So, it seems like an easy decision.

But I purposely avoid hiring from my competitors. Instead of direct experience, I look for transferable skills. Does someone I am considering hiring know how to solve problems? Can they initiate relationships easily? Do they have the potential to grow in our company? I have found that leadership ability and selling ability are transferable skills. I came out of the chemical industry and ended up in the car rental industry. Why? Because my leadership and relationship skills were transferable.

In most cases, you can learn the important nuances of a particular industry quickly. Leadership and sales skills, however, take a long time to develop—and you can carry them with you. That is the key. I prefer to hire intelligent people, with the right work ethic, skill set, and potential, who also understand our culture and want to be part of our mission, and then train them in the techniques they need to know about our industry.

TAKE THE TIME FOR RIGHT HIRES

The employee I hired at Avis to be my replacement as senior vice president of sales for the Americas was Beth Kinerk, who at the time was the senior vice president of sales and customer development at a Fortune 500 healthcare company. It took me over a year to bring her on as my replacement to head up sales when I became president of North America. One might not think that her background with a pharmaceutical services company would line her up to be an obvious first choice. However, her emotional maturity, and her understanding of how to connect with employees and customers, set her apart, along with her competitiveness, optimism, resilience, and grit.

As it turned out, she showed up for her hiring interview with me on the last day of our Bus Tour, as we pulled in to headquarters. She described that day from her perspective: "I was hooked when I felt the warmth of the reception he and his team received, and heard him command the room, as he spoke so passionately from the heart, with such authenticity and emotional candor."

Beth added, "From the start, I could see that the culture he was creating dismantled any kind of hierarchy and any focus on ego. His emphasis was on humility and integrity, and people were drawn to it naturally. So, for me, as a sales leader, I knew that would be easy for me to sell. We had something that separated us from the competition. And you could see that 'something' when you were on the other side of the desk from a customer."

When I initially interviewed Beth, I explored in depth how she would respond to this new situation. When I am looking to bring someone new into the organization, particularly in a high-profile position, I start by making sure that he or she will not just blend in but will also contribute in meaningful ways to the culture we are creating together. This is why you first need to be clear about the strengths and values that distinguish your organization. As I have emphasized, your values set you—and your organization—apart. You need to be crystal clear about them. Do you embody accountability, compassion, or competition? Is creativity, flexibility, or integrity what you stand for? Is your organization focused on making a difference, on optimism, or on relationships? When you are living your organization's core values, it makes it much easier for you to discern whether someone new will "fit in" or "stick out."

With Beth, I sensed an alignment of values. This read on her turned out to be true, as I saw firsthand after I hired her. As she said, "Ultimately, Tom and I shared many of the same attitudes and approaches toward the people we surround ourselves with. We celebrate their successes. But we also created a very high level of expectation. And we made decisions quickly and ran with them. We both had that same sense of urgency."

Whenever I feel that an external candidate's values are aligned with those of our organization, then I look to see if the individual's unique strengths are also aligned with the specific position. For Beth's position as a sales leader, I had a long, non-negotiable list of strengths, including openness to new ideas, competitiveness, confidence, creativity, curiosity, empathy, emotional maturity, enthusiasm, goal orientation, grit, inspiring others, optimism, passion, persuasiveness, resilience, self-awareness, self-discipline, team orientation, thriving under pressure, trust, and willingness to take risks.

There are personality assessments that can provide you with insights into whether a candidate possesses the strengths you are seeking. From there, you need to rely upon your interviewing skills and your internal compass. As the renowned author Peter Drucker said, "The best leaders ask the best questions." And they know what to listen for. What I want to uncover in an interview is whether an individual has a driving ambition to achieve. I am also interested to know how he or she has overcome failure. On the flip side of that, I want to know what the candidate considers to be the most significant achievement in his or her life. I also like to ask, "What one aspect of your current job would you eliminate, if you could?" If they want to get rid of a task that is key to the position you are seeking to fill, that may be all you need to know. In addition, I like them to tell me about the favorite part of their current job. Such questions will give you insights into the candidate. At the very least, they can tell you who to avoid.

Because the sales leadership position that Beth was applying for was so vital to the organization, I was not willing to compromise on someone who did not share our values and possess all the required strengths. That is why it took me over a year to find her.

I know that a year can seem like a very long time to be looking for someone to fill a key position in your organization, but it is worth waiting for the right person. I am keenly aware that patience in such a situation can be extremely difficult. That empty seat can be a constant reminder that something (and someone) is missing. Believe me, I get that. What is important to keep in mind, though, is that if you hire the wrong person, the damage to your organization's morale and bottom line can be extremely costly. And that time wasted can never be recouped. A hiring mistake is costly on so many levels.

Let's do the math. First, let's say it takes you three months to bring someone in from the outside for a key position. Even that would be extremely quick when you consider that advertisements need to be placed, applications screened, assessments taken, and initial interviews conducted over the phone, then several rounds of in-person interviews arranged for the final candidates with key colleagues inside the organization. Then, once an offer is made, the candidate you select likely will have to give several weeks' notice.

So, let's say you are very fortunate and you bring someone in from the outside in three months after the previous leader left the organization. Then, like most companies, you will give the new employee a standard ninety-day trial period. If at that point, you discover you have made a mistake and decide to part ways, you then have to start the hiring process all over again. This means another three months, at least, to find someone new, and that is if everything happens at an accelerated pace.

So, add it up. First, there are three months to bring the person who did not work out onboard. Then there are three months to realize you have made a mistake. Last, there are three more months to start the process all over and try to find someone else. That is nine months. Wasted. (And often it takes much longer to realize you have hired the wrong person, before you then try, once again, to find the right person.)

Here is how that translates: For three-quarters of a year your organization is left adrift, or, worse, is in turmoil. People are wondering (or doubting) that the new person will work out any better than the last one. And throughout that time, you are busy dealing with damage control—rather than focusing on new possibilities. That is why I always listen to my gut whenever I feel the slightest tinge of doubt about hiring someone from outside for an important position.

In Beth's case, my gut *and* my heart both agreed, resoundingly.

Shortly after she started, I remember Beth and her husband, Scott, were at our awards banquet. She said, "It was the first time my husband had ever been invited to a company function." I greeted them both and introduced them to others, and I recall Beth enthusing about a meeting she had just had where she felt a multimillion-dollar account was open to signing an exclusive agreement with us. At the time, that particular client was evenly contributing revenue derived from auto rentals to us as well as our two other key competitors.

I remember taking off my glasses and saying to Beth, "Look me in the eye." As she did, I said, "You do not have a snowball's chance in hell of getting an exclusive with this client." I paused, then added, "I just want to manage your expectations." Then I smiled at her, as I could see her competitive juices flowing.

"That was when I wanted to sign that agreement even more," Beth said. "It was a brilliant use of reverse psychology."

Beth and her team prepared for the next meeting with our client with a fervor that I had never seen before. In the presentation, she was like an orchestra conductor, bringing in world-class musicians to create an exceptional performance. Our head of operations, our head of fleet, and our head of customer service, one after the other, demonstrated our commitment to provide exemplary service and come through for our customers. She showed a video of The Bus Tour to convey the passion within our culture. Then she brought everyone down to the vestibule where she had a truck with the client's logo on it. Everyone in the room felt our commitment.

As Beth said, "We gave them reason after reason to join forces with us exclusively because we understood their needs and demonstrated that we were driven to be a true partner with them. It was one of the best collaborative deals I have ever been part of in my career." I can still remember the enthusiasm in her voice when she called me after she and her team were awarded the exclusive agreement. Later, when I asked our client's decision makers what we did for them to bestow upon us this unprecedented agreement, I was told, "Two things: we trusted your team, and we believed in our partnership together."

Leading with your heart starts with trust. Then you can build upon that trust. And everything becomes possible. With trust as your foundation, I encourage you, as a leader, to constantly look for potential in those around you. Have your antennae up for anyone in your organization who brings an interesting perspective. Then spend time with them. Lots of time. Listen to them. Ask them about their favorite parts of their current job. And their least favorite parts. What do those answers say about their future? Do they get lost in the details? Or can they connect the dots between what is and what can be? Do they understand how to develop deep relationships with others? Are they open to new ideas? Do you know their aspirations?

Then, if your heart tells you it is right, give them a challenging assignment that points in the direction they, and you, are seeking. Believe in them. And be there for them—*personally and professionally.*

THE LANGUAGE OF THE HEART

The words we choose say a lot about what is on our minds, as well as what is in our hearts. I find that much of the language of business—particularly when it comes to talking about people—is stiff and stifling.

LET'S GET REAL WITH OUR WORDS

Just consider for a moment some of the words that are commonly used when talking about people in an organization. Even the phrase "human resources" gets under my skin. We are not talking about resources. We are talking about *people*. I absolutely hate such phrases—along with "human capital" and "full-time equivalents" (which is some financial way of saying "a person").

Such phrases diminish the significance of people. I do not believe these words are chosen by accident. By referring to humans as *resources*, leaders allow themselves to think about (and, most importantly, *not feel* about) the people with whom they are working as assets that are deployable and expandable.

Such artificial language, I believe, diminishes the real significance of people. "Human resources" do not have wives, husbands, daughters, sons, parents, grandchildren, grandparents, friends, anniversaries, births, diseases, deaths, headaches, vacations, heartaches, challenges, or celebrations.

Words like "human resources" and "full-time equivalents" can provide leaders with a comfortable distance whenever they are making difficult decisions. Then, when there is a need for a layoff or downsizing, those who are "redundant" can be dismissed because they are "surplus to the requirements of the organization."

Those phrases are not just callous. Such language is insidious. Those words eat at the heart and soul of an organization, reinforcing a belief that human resources are transferable, disposable, and replaceable.

That is why when I hear leaders talk about "my direct reports" or "my subordinates," I will stop them midsentence and ask if they realize what they sound like by using such phrases. I ask if they have given any thought to what these words really mean. Then I ask if that is how they really want to think and feel about the people with whom they are working shoulder-to-shoulder. Is that their real intention? Just hearing the phrase "so-and-so works for me" drives me crazy. That sense of ownership and superiority is misguided, at best. At worst, it reinforces a sense that those around us are our possessions. People do not work for me. We work together.

Ultimately, my message is to talk about, think about, feel about, and believe in "people."

I believe in the language of the heart.

Collaboration is what unites a team. It is about "we."

My very strong advice is to eliminate from your vocabulary words like "full-time equivalents" and "heads"—even the phrase "human resources."

Let's drop those words. Let's be real.

THERE IS JUST "WE"

At Avis, multiple nationalities were represented in our organization. It was very important to me that we respected everything about each and every one of the individuals working with us—their religious beliefs, their cultural values, their sexual orientation, everything that made them who they are. It did not matter the color of their skin, the color of their hair, or the color of their eyes. What mattered was what was inside of them.

My message was to talk about and connect with "people."

Let's let everyone know that we care about them. Let's let them know that *they* are *us.* There is just "we." Let's respect everyone as family.

Let's start by using the words that express our feelings. Our language speaks volumes about who we are and what we believe.

So, let's talk from the heart.

RECOGNIZING THE POTENTIAL IN PEOPLE: QUESTIONS FOR SELF-EVALUATION

The questions we ask ourselves, and how deeply we answer them, help to shape who we become. With that in mind, I encourage you to dive deeply as you explore these questions. Then review your answers from time to time. And allow your answers to evolve. Your answers will serve as road signs on your leadership journey.

1. Are you open to thinking about someone's potential, to seeing them in a new light?
2. How do you identify the potential in someone else?
3. Do you know the qualities that distinguish your top performers? Do you know what drives them— and where that drive can take them?
4. What do you know about your organization's high-potential individuals on a personal level? Do you understand the desires, needs, inhibitors to growth, and aspirations of your top talent?
5. Have you built a development plan for your top performers that aligns their aspirations with the organization's goals? Are you recognizing and rewarding them? Are you letting them know how important they are to your organization?
6. What is your talent management process like?

7. How open and honest are your conversations with people about their strengths and their ability to grow?
8. What can you do when someone plateaus?
9. Do you use personality assessments or some other objective criteria in your hiring process?
10. Do you seek the advice of others?
11. Do you listen to what you may not want to hear regarding a promising candidate about whom you are enthused?
12. Is there diversity of skills and thinking on your team that are complementary to one another?
13. How do you work around someone's personal issues (e.g., major life events, such as a birth, serious illness, or death in the family)?
14. How can you identify future needs for your organization—in a world that is ever changing?

CHAPTER 7

DELIVERING TOUGH NEWS
WITH YOUR HEART

When your heart is open, you can have honest and trusting conversations with people, connecting on a deep level about ideas, feelings, events, issues, concerns that really matter. Such conversations make life interesting, meaningful, and fun.

But how can you maintain that same level of openness, honesty, and trust when the conversations become personally or professionally difficult?

How can you have such difficult conversations (which you might just as easily avoid) in a way that is equally caring, sincere, and candid?

Is there a way to have these conversations with love in your heart?

What matters most when you are having a difficult conversation with someone you care about is that trust, honesty, openness, and compassion are at the foundation of your relationship.

Forthright conversations are vital for an organization to thrive. Yet most of us shy away from having difficult conversations. We do not want to hurt anyone's feelings. In fact, many leaders default to keeping a safe distance between themselves and those around them because they do not want to find themselves in the awkward position of having a difficult conversation with someone who has become a friend. They feel that blending their professional and personal relationships could be a slippery slope.

Adam Johnson, the chairman and CEO of NetJets, and a colleague and friend with whom I have collaborated on several opportunities that have helped both of our organizations, emphasized, "I've seen people at all levels of an organization falter because they do not know how to have difficult conversations with their colleagues. As a result, they can either deny the truth or hammer it. Then they wonder why they are not able to effectuate the change they need to occur."

For me, however, keeping a "safe distance" is not an option. I prefer to go in the exact opposite direction. What you'll find in developing closer relationships with your colleagues is worth so much more than what is lost in keeping a safe distance.

Still, it takes care and courage to have difficult conversations with love in your heart. Interestingly, the word "courage" comes from the Latin word *cor*, which means "heart." Leading with heart takes an inner strength.

What matters in this interaction with someone you care about is that there is trust, honesty, openness, and compassion at the foundation of your relationship. Experience has shown me that if your relationship has honesty and trust as its foundation, you can have difficult conversations in a way that is caring and sincere, with the best interests of the individual and your organization at heart. This is true whether your relationship is personal, professional, or a blend of both.

Sometimes when we have these challenging conversations, we might even be pleasantly surprised at the outcome. I've had several difficult conversations with individuals that surprised and transformed them—personally and professionally.

BEING TRUTHFUL, OPEN, HONEST, COMPASSIONATE, *AND* FIRM

Just because I have been emphasizing succeeding through the depth of your connections, that does not mean that I am talking about taking a soft and easy route. I am firm about holding myself, and those with whom I surround myself, completely accountable. This is an extremely important distinction to keep in mind.

Leading with heart is about openly and honestly recognizing the talent and potential of those around you, while also acknowledging and addressing any concerns as soon as they occur. That last part is where difficult conversations need to happen—with courage and compassion.

It is important to underscore that leading with your heart is *not* about avoiding difficult conversations. Quite the contrary. It is about having those conversations in a way that honestly connects, with compassion and clarity, aiming to create a desired outcome.

Still, let's face it: it can be very challenging to have a difficult conversation with someone you care about. I have come to realize that I am able to have such conversations precisely because I do care. I know that *how* something is told—with concern and understanding—can make all the difference in the world when you are having a tough conversation with someone. That is why I am completely clear with the truth—even if it is bad news—so that someone can digest it and know what they are dealing with. I have learned that what is most important is to tell the unvarnished truth in a straightforward way that lets someone realize that, even though they do not like what they are hearing, they are in a position to change things for the better. That is how I have moved organizations forward—one person and one conversation at a time.

On a personal note, my son Kevin, who is the chief financial officer of All American Title, as well as an entrepreneur who has speculated extremely well on land purchases, said that while growing up, he realized that central to all my conversations was "the goal." He explained, "My dad sees the goal with enormous clarity—no matter how far away it might be. And he understands what needs to be done to get there. That is why, I believe, he is able to make someone feel important and special when they are succeeding. Then, with that same belief in each individual, he is able to close the door and have a difficult conversation when it is needed. It is that mentoring that he does so well and why he can help people discover something inside themselves that they didn't realize was there. And it is done with the same belief in the person—whether the conversation is encouraging or cautionary.

"If there is something my dad sees that is not going right, he will deal with it right away, rather than let it fester. He has the confidence (and stomach) to deal with problems, which a lot of people just do not. So, they will often shy away from those hard conversations that can make them feel so uncomfortable. But, for my dad, it is all about reaching the goal—together. That is how he delivers his messages. Even the more difficult ones. And, for those who are ready, such conversations can open them up to very important learning experiences. They just need to remember, as he does, that it is ultimately all about the goal. I know a lot of people do not know how to separate their personal thoughts and feelings from what it takes in the moment to achieve their goal. But my dad sees that all very clearly."

Kevin smiled, then added, "Growing up, I had great training courses in leadership at our dinner table. My dad would talk very openly with us about his successes and concerns at work. We all knew the key players and what was going on. I believe that is why I felt a little better prepared than most people my age to enter the workforce and succeed. I learned to be clear about the goal. And to be open, caring, and compassionate with everyone on our team as we collaborated together to succeed."

With that in mind, let me share a difficult conversation I had with Andre Meesschaert.

Some people are big. And then there is Andre. Let's just say that if we were playing a friendly game of touch football, I would want Andre on my team. With him blocking everyone in front of me, I could score easily. Andre is six feet three inches tall. And when I met him, he tipped the scales at four hundred pounds.

Andre is truly an international citizen, having been born in the United Kingdom, then having lived in Belgium, France, Canada, and the United States. I believed he could grow with our company. So, after I became president of North America for Avis Budget Group, I approached Andre with the possibility of a promotion. Then I looked him in the eye, and said, "In order to take on this promotion, Andre, you have to do something for me." I paused, then added, 'You have to promise me that you will lose weight.'

He was quite taken aback. "For many years," Andre related, "I was extremely overweight. But my problem was that I did not have any health problems because of it. I just was not able to sit in an economy seat on a plane and I had to buy my clothes at a specialty shop. But I was using food as a way of coping with stress, and it seemed to work for me. Then here was Tom going to a place where nobody had ever gone before."

I shared with Andre that I was talking from my own personal experience. I told him, "It dawned on me when I was watching a video of my son's wedding, and I thought, 'Who is that big fat guy dancing with my wife? That can't be me.'"

I told him that after that, I lost about eighty-five pounds. Then I added, "I've experienced it. And it is not good for you or your family. I did it. You can do it. Losing weight will give you more confidence. It'll make everything better." Then I added, "I believe in you, I want to help groom your talent. But I really want to make sure that our investment will pay off and that you will not collapse on me and end up in a hospital a year or two from now."

The reason I was able to broach this subject with Andre was *because I truly cared about him on a personal level, first and foremost*. Certainly, I saw him as someone with amazing talent and potential who could help our organization succeed at a new level. But, most importantly, I cared about him personally, and connected with him on a deep, emotional level. So, I saw this difficult conversation as my responsibility—because I was truly fond of and concerned for him.

As Andre said, "Nobody had ever talked with me like that before. He has the guts to go places no one else will go. The conversation was person-to-person—not president-to-director. He just put a message across that 'You've got to do this. And you can do this.' It was a hard message. But I could not argue the facts. And I was left thinking, 'Here is a great opportunity career-wise. And if I say 'yes,' I cannot rely on my old excuses any more. If I say 'yes,' I am making a commitment. It all came down to Tom having a very hard conversation with me, then following through with love. I never really used that word before in a business setting. But I learned to from Tom. I started to appreciate what love really meant after working with him."

He added, "More than anything else, Tom taught me that, as a leader, I need to start by being open and vulnerable with the people around me. To talk honestly, genuinely, and truthfully about what I believe in. That is what people want to hear. That is who they want to follow."

Over time, Andre lost almost half of his weight. He went from four hundred to two hundred and twenty pounds. "Beyond that," Andre added, "I was not expecting how my confidence, my ability to express myself, and my ability to think clearly would improve so much afterward. I was still the person I was before, but I started changing. I changed how I thought about myself. I changed how I thought about life in general. And about how I saw new opportunities."

The transformation in Andre alone has made my career as a leader worthwhile. He is now heading up European operations for Avis Budget Group. And he just ran in the New York Marathon. In fact, about five times during the marathon, he said, "I 'pulled a Gartland.'"

"Pulled a Gartland?" I asked.

Laughing, as though he had just disclosed a secret, he said, "Yeah. Tom would often get to feeling so emotionally involved in what he was talking about that he would just start tearing up. He would do it in individual meetings or in front of five hundred people. So, on the one hand, he is a big guy, who can be very intimidating. But he can also tear up in a moment's notice. So, that became known as 'pulling a Gartland.' It is a rare quality. The depth of his feelings just comes out because he truly cares."

Andre added, "So, there I was running a marathon, which I would have never done if it had not been for Tom. And I 'pulled a Gartland.' About five times during the run, I just started crying. Because I could not believe I was really doing it. These emotions came over me. And I am in the middle of about fifty thousand runners crying my eyes out like a baby." Andre paused, then added, "That's another thing I would have never, *ever* done if I had not met Tom. He has shown me how a leader can help you get in touch with your true feelings and realize your true potential—professionally and personally."

Some people, upon hearing this story, are incredulous, asking if I was not afraid of being sued. Others ask if I would be willing to have a similar conversation with a woman.

The answers to those questions are no and yes, in that order.

I was not concerned about being sued by Andre because I had come to know him over the course of several years, and we had developed a deep and abiding trust in each other. And I have had as many difficult conversations with women as I have with men.

What matters is the trust and understanding that underlies such conversations. Still, such conversations can be difficult. I just accept that as an essential part of leading. What matters most is that the conversation is conducted in a very straightforward and honest way, with an underlying belief that we have each other's backs. Ultimately, when it came to what conversations to have, I would always do what was best for the organization. To me, there is a basic honesty, integrity, clarity, and responsibility in this approach.

YOUR WORDS AND ACTIONS SET THE EXPECTATIONS

Leading is about guiding outcomes. And if we want those around us to believe in us, we need to guide them when they are off track, just as we need to recognize and reward them when they are doing very well.

Here is my premise: *Everyone in the organization knows what is going on.* They know who is excelling, just as they are aware of who is coasting. And, as a leader, they are looking to you to see what you do (or don't do) about people in both categories. Your actions and words in both situations set the tone for what is expected. The worst thing is when honest conversations are not taking place. That can lead nowhere—for the individual in question and the organization at large.

My philosophy is that everyone in the organization is watching what you do, and what you don't do. Your words and actions set the expectations. So, if someone is not measuring up, and you are letting the situation drag on, everyone gets the message that you will allow such behavior and performance to linger. Meanwhile, if you are fair and honest with the individual and come to a decision that is right for the organization, then you are sending a message that you are living by your principles and your values.

That is why I do not hesitate to have a straightforward conversation with someone whom I believe in, but who needs to improve in some area. What matters is that such conversations are delivered with dignity and compassion. It is vital to have such conversations in ways that let the individual know that I respect, value, and am still there for him or her. And I confirm that my hope is that he or she will be able to turn the situation around.

At such times, one approach I have found to be helpful is to have more than one voice involved. This is where a 360 evaluation can be helpful by pulling together multiple voices and perspectives. Then, when the individual sees a consistency to the message, it might open him or her up to a breakthrough. At that time, a coach might also be very helpful if you are trying to bring that situation around. But it takes a breakthrough on the part of the individual, who needs to recognize that he or she has a real concern and is ready to make some needed changes.

It might be that they are not collaborating with their colleagues. They may have become more negative and critical than they were before. Perhaps they are not coming through on their commitments. Whatever the concern is, they need to recognize it, do some real soul searching, and turn the situation *and themselves* around.

Such situations can go either way—depending upon the individual's openness to change.

But if the individual cannot make whatever adjustments are necessary to improve his or her performance, then they have made my choice clear. I would then have such discussions with compassion and generosity. And I would hope to maintain our friendship and help them in whatever way I could. But, at the end of the day, I would always do what was best for the business.

There was a good friend I had to let go once, and it was very difficult for me because I cared for him deeply. But,

after several coaching conversations with very little changing, I knew that letting him go was the right decision for the
organization. And he took it hard. Very hard. He was bright,
had solid values, was well-liked, and gave it his all. But the
organization he was overseeing for us at the time was in the
midst of huge changes, and he was not decisive enough to
run it. So, he was not the right person at that time, that's all.
Still, I knew that being let go hurt him immensely. And such
wounds can take time to heal. In fact, recently I received a
phone call from him asking how my wife and I were doing.
Then he thanked me for helping him land a different position, which I did when he left. He closed by saying that he
would like to stay in touch. So I was more than glad to catch
up on how he was doing. We had a very nice conversation,
but it took time for that to happen. I understand that. Ultimately, I trust and believe that life has a way of working
things out.

EVERYONE'S UNIQUE CAREER PATHS

It is important to recognize that everyone's career path
depends upon a unique combination of their talents, abili-
ties, potential, energy, and drive while also depending upon
the unique needs of their ever-changing organization. This
is true regardless of how long someone has been with an
organization.

Life would be a lot easier if our careers all progressed
smoothly and upward. But due to circumstances that are

often beyond our control, there are times when this is not the case. There are times in our lives when change is needed to align ourselves with what is going on around us.

Like it was yesterday, I remember speaking with compassion to an executive who had been with our organization for a long time. I shared with him that we were creating a position for him where he would have fewer people reporting to him but he would be using his talents and insights to help grow the potential of some of our newest employees, which had become a major strategic initiative for our organization. The executive was taken aback, even though in several previous conversations I had prepared him for such a move. Still, I knew, this was a major shift for him because his previous title was such an essential part of his identity. Ultimately, however, he came to appreciate that I believed in and was there for the organization—*and* for him. And he came to realize that this change could open him up to a new perspective about himself and those around him.

Six months into his new position, he shared with me that he realized he was a "blocker" in his previous position. I asked him what he meant by that term, and he said that he had come to understand that, while his career had progressed nicely and smoothly for a long time, he realized he had plateaued. When that happens to a senior member of the team, he continued, all the younger people with real growth potential are saying, "If this guy's not going anywhere, then where is my career going?" Then he said that the whole organization would begin to decay if there was no opportunity for those coming up to continue to grow.

I complimented him on his perception, self-awareness, and how, by adapting to this new position, he was truly helping the organization in ways that were needed and would have an enormous impact on our future. Later that day, I smiled, recalling the conversation, and realized that his reflections reinforced the message that for us, as leaders, we do not need to be concerned about getting close to the people around us. Quite the contrary. They need to know where we stand, and what we stand for. They have to believe that they are on solid ground. They want to feel part of something bigger than themselves. And they desire to experience the depth of real connections.

Truly connecting with those around you means being honest—about them and about how they are fitting (or not) into the organization as it (and they) move forward.

There are certainly times when conversations about an individual's career can be as wonderful and exciting as a champagne toast. Then, there are other times when those conversations can be as difficult and challenging as a farewell hug.

What you ultimately find in developing closer relationships with your colleagues is worth so much more than what is lost in keeping a safe distance. That is why leading with your heart can be fulfilling and challenging. It can be daunting and rewarding. It takes a personal commitment, integrity, trust, energy, and openness to have whatever conversations are needed at the time. Leading with your heart means being honest with yourself and with those around you, and then acting on your honest realizations.

It all comes back around, once again, to *Words Plus Actions Matching*.

In the end, such openness, compassion, and honesty can create a culture that attracts truly talented individuals—because they believe in the values you stand for, they believe they can thrive in such an environment, and they believe in the organization's future.

HOW CAN YOU COACH OTHER LEADERS IN YOUR ORGANIZATION TO HAVE DIFFICULT CONVERSATIONS WITH COMPASSION?

A key part of leading with your heart is coaching other leaders to feel comfortable getting their points across to everyone on their team in clear, open, honest, and caring ways that create desired results. The goal is for everyone to know what they need to do to keep their careers and the organization moving forward. With that as your premise, you can then connect more deeply with your team while holding yourself and everyone else accountable.

Connecting more deeply while holding everyone on your team accountable are two sides of the same coin. That is why, when someone on your team is not living up to expectations, it is your responsibility to have a difficult conversation. Your hope is that the single conversation alone will take care of the concern. But, depending upon the individual's level of self-awareness and desire to change, one conversation may become several, leading to a foregone conclusion.

Such forthright conversations often can be particularly difficult for new managers, who may cringe at the idea of having a tough talk with someone on their team. So what steps can a new manager take to overcome their natural concerns and have open, honest, and productive conversations about difficult subjects?

STEP 1: DETERMINE THE VALUE OF THE CONVERSATION FOR THE ORGANIZATION

Ask yourself: *Why is this conversation important for our organization?* Take the time to write out your thoughts. Outline the key points you need to get across. Get clear about the message you want to deliver and why, then convey it convincingly, along with the results you seek.

STEP 2: UNDERSTAND THE RECIPIENT'S PERSPECTIVE

Be empathetic. To feel connected with the other person, you want to understand his or her feelings. Ask yourself: *If I were receiving this message, how would I want it to be delivered? What is it like to be in his or her shoes?*

STEP 3: COMBINE CONTENT WITH CARE

Blend the key points you need to make with the connection you feel with the person. Don't let your feelings confuse your message. You can be personal without taking this personally. Be able to answer the question: *How can I deliver my message with care and compassion, while also being clear about what I am saying and why?*

STEP 4: PRACTICE

Rehearse your conversation. Try it out with someone close to you, whom you trust as a partner. This of course needs to be someone who you can be completely confident will not let a word out, whose experience and insights you respect, and who can advise you about conveying your message more effectively.

STEP 5: SET UP A TIME TO TALK

After you have taken in all you need from the first four steps, arrange a time to have the conversation. There is no benefit in delaying the inevitable.

STEP 6: DELIVER YOUR WORDS WITH INTENTION

Be very intentional when you have the conversation. Let the individual know that you believe in them and in their ability to make the necessary change. Realize that while this conversation might be difficult for the person to take in at this point, he or she will carry it with them. They will play it over and over again in their mind and their heart. And even though he or she might not like what is being said at the time, if the conversation is done with empathy and with concern and with your heart open, they will recognize this.

STEP 7: CONNECT

What matters, ultimately, is how something is done. That is what they will remember. Your intent is to deliver a message in such a way that it connects with the individual—now and later. And your hope is that he or she can bring about the desired change. Meanwhile, your entire team is watching how you handle this conversation. So, realize that you are delivering this message personally—as well as universally.

It is certainly easier to deliver good news with love in your heart. Delivering news that is difficult to hear with love in your heart, however, is the sign of a true leader.

WOMEN AND MEN NEED TO BE EQUALLY FREE TO LEAD WITH HEART

It is very interesting to me to see the reactions of some people when they see me start to tear up and hug someone as I thank them for doing a great job. I know that can have different meanings for people based on where they are coming from.

Some people compliment me for being so open and honest, then go on to share something about themselves that they have not said previously, or for a long time. And yet I realize it can make some people uncomfortable. Some women have shared that because I am, as Andre said, "a big guy, who can be very intimidating," that my tearing up is something that women in our society do not have the luxury of doing, for fear that their crying would confirm cultural perceptions that they are "too emotional" to be an effective leader.

I appreciate how some people applaud what I am doing (simply being myself) because they feel that I am bucking expectations. So, without meaning to, I get an extra point for that. But I also understand that for female leaders, being open about their emotions could be viewed as just confirming a stereotype—and some people take off a point for that. I get that. And it bothers me. Immensely.

The notion that women today are still caught in this no-win situation offends me. These prejudices show that we still have a long way to evolve. So, let me emphasize by saying out loud that leaders (regardless of gender) are more effective when we are allowed to be open about our thoughts, feelings, and actions. There ought to be no differences in how we view female or male leaders—except in how effective they are.

Still, I recognize that, depending upon the audience, male leaders may have an unfair advantage in expressing our emotions. By being open and personal, some may see us as somehow being secure within ourselves. Meanwhile, a female leader who expresses her emotions too freely can run the risk of being seen as confirming a stereotype because she is not able to "control" her emotions.

That unfair comparison, I feel, is patently unjust and unequivocally wrong. It is the exact opposite of what I am advocating for all of us.

To the extent that I am given a free pass to step safely outside of convention and express my deepest emotions in the workplace—simply because of my gender—and that women are confined to withhold their emotions because they may not be seen as strong leaders shows that we, as a society, have much work to do.

I hope that at least by engaging in this conversation we can help to change the outcome.

CREATING A POSITIVE AURA AROUND EMOTIONS

Gina Bruzzichesi, the former senior vice president at Avis Budget Group and now senior vice president of global operations for WeWork, confirmed that "as a female in a very male-dominated industry, I struggled to find mentors. I remember trying to mimic the style of different leaders throughout my career. And it always led me away from myself—because my style was so much more intimate and personal. The very clear message they were sending me was not to let my guard down and to dial back my emotions."

She added, "With Tom, I allowed myself to become more vulnerable because I knew he respected that in himself and in others. He created a positive aura around emotions. And that allowed women and men to flourish as leaders, rather than have to hide our emotions behind some wall that we built to protect ourselves."

What is required, I would argue, is for us as leaders, regardless of gender, to embrace a culture that allows our thoughts and feelings to flourish. If we are not being whole, we are not being ourselves. And leading, I firmly believe, requires us to be all of ourselves.

BEING TRUE TO OURSELVES

Barbara Kogen, who was the vice president of organizational development and performance for Avis Budget Group, said, "At the end of the day, people connect with leaders who are true to themselves. If women are afraid to lead from the heart, then we are doing ourselves a disservice. We will not come across as authentic. *We need to open our hearts and let people see who we are, while also holding ourselves and others accountable.* That is the balance that is needed in any leader today."

It is not an either/or. Being a leader means having a tough skin while also thinking and feeling deeply. It is about crying sometimes and being tough as nails other times. Leading is about opening ourselves, and those around us, up to new possibilities.

It all starts by sharing who we are.

DELIVERING TOUGH NEWS WITH YOUR HEART: QUESTIONS FOR SELF-EVALUATION

The questions we ask ourselves, and how deeply we answer them, help to shape who we become. With that in mind, I encourage you to dive deeply as you explore these questions. Then review your answers from time to time. And allow your answers to evolve. Your answers will serve as road signs on your leadership journey.

1. Do you have the courage to have a difficult conversation with a colleague? Or do you avoid such conversations?
2. Are you having the conversation in the context of what is best for the company?
3. When you are having a difficult conversation with someone, is your tendency to come down too hard on them?
4. When you have to address what needs to change in an individual, are you specific, or are you inclined to be a bit too vague?
5. If the person you are having a difficult conversation with gets emotional, can you keep your emotions out of it?
6. Can you have a difficult conversation with empathy—placing yourself in the other person's shoes? Do you consider how you would want this message delivered to you?

7. Can you see yourself as a mentor when you are having a difficult conversation?

8. Have you hypothesized the conversation? Have you role-played the conversation? What could happen?

9. When you need to let someone go, how can you do it in the most humane, caring way?

CHAPTER 8

CREATING A PURPOSE AND STRATEGY THAT CONNECTS WITH YOUR TEAM

My daughter Sara is a professional opera singer. I have heard her and other professional musicians talk about playing from the neck up or the neck down. What they mean is that performing "serious" music can be technically demanding. Accurately playing the right notes at the right time with the right rhythm is what they call playing from the neck up. But the feeling that moves you in a piece of music is visceral. That is playing from the neck down. As audience members, we feel the difference when a musician is playing just from the neck up. We may be impressed by his or her technique, but we are truly moved when a musician plays from the neck down as well.

Leading at its best, I have found, is similar to music in this way. Like musicians, we want to lead from the neck up and the neck down. That is where and when we are truly connecting—with ourselves and with others.

DO YOU KNOW YOUR "WHY"?

While my emphasis is on people, I believe that succeeding in business starts with a compelling purpose and a clearly articulated strategy. This is where you, as a leader, need to connect your head with your heart, your purpose with your beliefs. Those you are leading need to believe in your purpose—the reason your organization exists. Why is what you are doing so important? Why is what you provide far superior to the product or services of your competitors? What difference are you making in the lives of your customers?

Your purpose needs to be significant and to capture the imagination of those around you. *Inspiring others is literally breathing life into your purpose.* That is when others will lean in to hear how they can contribute in meaningful ways to a purpose that is important. Then, with their hearts, they will agree to sign on for the journey.

Once your purpose is embraced, your strategy sets the direction, defining how, together, you will come through for your customers, be there for your colleagues, compete in the marketplace, and achieve your goals. Your strategy gets to the heart of what you believe in and why. It lets everyone know how, together, you will reach your goals, and what

guiding principles you will all rely upon when vital decisions need to be made quickly, in the face of uncertainty.

Your strategy is not a document that can be created and
tucked away in some drawer. It needs to be reviewed and
fine-tuned on an ongoing basis, and it must stay flexible
enough to be adapted to the constantly changing marketplace. What is working? What is not? And why?

*For others to follow you, they need to believe in three
things: you, your organization's purpose, and your strategy
for succeeding.* Do they believe they can trust you? Do they
believe what you are doing together is important? And do
they believe in your master plan? When the answers to those
three questions are *yes, yes,* and *yes*—then the right people
will be drawn to your organization, enthused to be part of
the journey's success, knowing they can play a vital role.

I am an advisor to and board member of several companies, and whenever I look inside an organization, my
questions always start in the same place: What is the organization's purpose? Is it powerful? Is the strategy clear? Do
people understand their role in executing the strategy? Is it
communicated in an inspiring way? I want to know what
distinguishes this organization. Does everyone know how
they are going to win? And do they believe it?

I have seen far too many leaders come into an organization and get this backward. They do not understand the
need for a clearly articulated purpose and a compelling
strategy to guide their decisions. So, they mistakenly start
"optimizing" or "creating efficiencies," which are just code

words for "making cuts." To me, that is the exact opposite of leading. And it is why their time as leaders is short.

Before a leader starts making major decisions, the people following him or her need to know why those decisions are being made—and those reasons need to be better than just to save money. Otherwise, everyone in the organization will respond in fear. Tensions will rise as doubt permeates. Then some individuals will duck for cover as others argue. Some will prepare their exit strategy, while others triple-check their work, worried about making mistakes. Not believing the organization has a strategy for growth, people understandably will be afraid that they will be among the next round of "cuts." Without a clear strategy, known to and understood by all, your organization will be fraught with confusion, division, and conflict.

Your success as a leader hinges on your ability to convey your organization's unique purpose, then create energy and momentum around your strategy in a compelling way. That is when the people around you will believe and begin to see new possibilities in themselves and those around them.

UNDERSTANDING YOUR ORGANIZATION'S PURPOSE

One of the most exemplary examples I have ever come across of a leader who has a clear understanding of his company's purpose is Chris McIntyre, CEO and cofounder of Eagle Rider. His organization began with four Harley-Davidsons in a garage in San Pedro, California. With Eagle Rider rapidly expanding throughout Europe, Asia, and Central America, Chris asked me to join his board of directors. While you could accurately describe Eagle Rider as the world's largest motorcycle tourism company, Chris said he is not really in the motorcycle business. Smiling, he added, "We are in the *experience* business. We rent dreams."

Just listen to how Chris explained why he, his colleagues, and his customers ride motorcycles: "There is a raw and visceral feeling to riding a bike in nature. It is a journey. You are no longer covered by metal and glass. You are just on two wheels, smelling the sage, feeling the sun on your forearms, sensing it will rain before you start to get wet. It is seeing, hearing, feeling, and all of your senses are open. That's what the experience is about. We are providing the opportunity for our customers to create their own destination and choose how they will get there."

That is a leader who knows how to express his organization's purpose, as he passionately paints a picture of the experience that connects him with his colleagues and his customers. Not surprisingly, the key members of Chris's team are all enthusiasts, embodying the same exuberant feeling that they eagerly provide to their customers. I encourage you to describe your organization's purpose with the same sense of inspiration and enthusiasm that Chris engenders. That is how you will attract the right people to your organization.

In our first conversation, he recognized, "As we grow exponentially, I need to look into the future of people—those with us now, and those who might join us for the journey." Chris added, "I need to surround myself with people who are equally passionate about our purpose, and who want to keep growing personally and professionally. That is the only way we will succeed." Agreeing completely, I added that what he had just described were individuals with a unique combination of personality qualities.

As we reviewed his organization's new growth possibilities, and talked about who on his team had the potential to step up and oversee new responsibilities, I said, "As you look at your team, you want to ask yourself whether someone who is very good at what he or she is doing now will be able to contribute in new ways as your organization experiences the changes that will come with dramatic growth. Among the questions you want to ask is, *Do they have the 'emotional maturity' to navigate those changes?*"

Chris asked me to explain what I meant by that phrase, and I said, "An organization like yours, which is growing at such an accelerated rate, can be exhilarating for some people, while also being disconcerting for others. You might see, as the organization changes, that some people feel like they are losing control of what they believe to be their 'power,' so they may start to resist the changes. Such individuals won't just get stuck in their ways; they will actually backslide. They don't intend to be that way. But they cannot stop themselves. Too much change makes them uncomfortable.

"While you can understand their resistance, those are not the individuals who can help you create the future. What you need, particularly now, as your organization is growing at such a rapid pace, is to surround yourself with individuals who believe in themselves as much as they believe in each other and the organization's purpose—and who embrace rapid change."

Then I added, "This is just one thing to be aware of. You are looking for talented individuals who have that special combination."

That special combination happens when your purpose is clear and embraced by the right people and their heart is in the game. By connecting your head with your heart, you are ready to focus intently on the people in your organization. With curiosity, compassion, and openness, you can then ask: Do you have the right people in place to make the strategy come alive? Are they in the right roles, with responsibilities that match their talents? Are they in positions that also challenge them? Do they thrive on collaborating? What is their potential? Do you have a plan for where they are going next? And who will take their place when they grow into new positions?

The questions you need to ask yourself about people can only be answered correctly after you have a clear purpose and strategy. That is why I believe in purpose, strategy, and people—in that order.

YOU NEED A REASON TO BELIEVE

When I took over as president of North America for Avis Budget Group, we were still recovering from the economic downturn of the Great Recession. I knew I had to give everyone within our organization a reason to believe.

For me, focusing on people became not only a personal value; it was a strategic choice. I believed there was an unmistakable connection between how we opened our hearts to each other as colleagues and how we could share that same depth of compassion with our customers.

My goal was to bring service distinctiveness back to life within the organization that was known for *trying harder*. That strategy—connecting our past with who we could become—became our road map. It was reinforced by making sure that we had the right people in the right positions to make that strategy come alive.

While that approach might sound very straightforward and deceptively simple, it requires some very important, and often difficult, decisions. Implementing your strategy involves making key choices about, and often significant changes in, the people on your team. You need to answer some very large questions, including: Who is in the right place now? Who is ready to move up? Who might not fit into the new plan? And do I need to bring someone new into the organization for a key position?

The decisions you make will have an enormous impact—personally and professionally—on everyone in your organization. Some will be very pleased. And others will be disappointed. Regardless of whether they agree or not, what everyone wants to know is that the decisions you are making about people are strategically driven and consistent with your purpose. Then, everyone will know what they need to do to step up their performance and be considered for a promotion the next time around.

As we began moving talented people into new positions that played to their strengths and aligned with our purpose and strategy, Ron Nelson, who was chairman of Avis Budget Group at the time, observed, "I have seen Tom cry in front of employees because of something touching or meaningful that happened. Still, I have seen him make very tough calls with what appears to be surprising ease."

How am I able to make those tough calls in one moment, then tear up a moment later because I had just met an employee who came through with flying colors? I know some leaders who prefer to emphasize accountability, setting a firm tone about what is expected, while others lean toward creating a more positive culture that recognizes and rewards those who exceed expectations. To me, it is all one and the same. There is no difference. Holding everyone accountable, while honoring those who bring out the best in us, is how we as leaders connect our heads with our hearts.

What matters is that it is clear to everyone that the changes you make are consistent with your values, your purpose, and your strategy.

ASSESSING YOUR PEOPLE

All too often I have seen leaders make important decisions about moving people into new positions based on nothing more than their gut feelings or the strong advice of someone in their executive circle.

To gain a broader and wider perspective about someone's potential, you need to have a rigorous process for assessing your talent, as well as clarity about what talent is needed for the future of your organization. That is why you need to know, empirically, what distinguishes your top performers. What qualities do they have that others lack? And how can you identify someone who has the potential to become such a top performer?

As a starting point, at Avis we created a benchmark of our top performers by matching their personality strengths with their performance reviews and their career aspirations. We were then able to view each of our top performers from various perspectives—including where they were at the time, how we could help them meet their goals, and where we saw them moving next, with an eye even further down the road.

In the back of my mind, I always needed to be aware of what we would do if anything happened to any of our top performers. Our company's success was based on my having a clear understanding of who the next leadership team would be. Who could be next in line? We needed to be sure that we were putting our people in the right roles along the way and developing their skills so that they were ready to step up when we went through a promotion process.

With a clear understanding of the organization's purpose and strategy, I believe your most important job as a leader is to develop individualized plans for each of your top performers that build into an overall succession plan.

Recognizing and developing your talent needs to be in the forefront of your mind as a leader. I can remember giving an enormous amount of thought to one of our best account managers, who was in her late twenties. The next promotional decision we would make for her potentially could influence her career for the next two decades—and affect our company for just as long. So, I knew that we had to get that right. We had to be committed to her. *As a leader, I believe it is my job to identify our most talented individuals, then grow the hell out of them.*

Sure, it is fun to recognize and reward your top performers. That is one of my absolute favorite things to do. Just as important, though, is being able to have a heart-to-heart conversation with someone who is not living up to expectations. I see both possible outcomes as two sides of the same coin.

WHAT IS WORKING, AND WHAT IS NOT?

Shedding light on what is and is not working is your job as a leader. So long as you are being fair and transparent in how you measure performance, then the results will speak for themselves. I believe in casting light on the truth, then making decisions based on what is clearly visible.

Stephen Wright, who is now senior vice president of global travel, partnerships, associations, and government at Avis Budget Group, shared how, as he said, I "changed our sales culture to reflect more accountability and more recognition."

He said, "Tom brought a boxing ringside bell into headquarters, which he hung outside of the boardroom, and he would ring it every time there was a huge sale. Then he created a Leader Board, where everyone could see how each sales team was performing compared with our revenue goals. And each time a region achieved an additional million dollars in sales revenue, the leader was invited to ring the bell for his or her team."

He smiled, then added, "When we brought on Air Canada, I got to ring the bell fifteen times for that one account. Tom would do that every Friday afternoon. And everyone in the building—from operations, finance, sales, marketing, and customer service—would all come up to celebrate our wins for that week. He got everyone engaged and involved in the excitement of each win. And his message was clear: those wins were about all of us winning.

"At the same time, Tom implemented Monthly Calls—where each leader talked about the new customers our team had brought on board, as well as any risks in our region. So, everything was out in the open. It was like having a business review every month. This did two things. It weeded out any poor performers. Because every month they were held accountable. At the same time, each month, the top performers were all striving to be recognized by Tom. And he would have these entertaining little side bets, with prizes like a new pair of shoes or cufflinks or a tie, just something to make it fun.

"By the third month, it was clear that this is how we were going to run and manage our business. And when we got into the flow of that, we really started succeeding. It made us all more accountable and successful. He did this in a way that motivated us by creating a culture of accountability and recognition. And the best salespeople thrived—because, by our nature, we are driven to be part of a culture of success."

As I implemented this strategy, the company's chairman, Ron Nelson, noted, "No one was confused about what they needed to accomplish under Tom's leadership. He created clear goals, then persistently followed up. He was almost relentless in that regard. Then he organized and energized people around initiatives through his unique relationship-building skills. It was a perfect blend."

You can have more accountability *and* more recognition. Top performers are motivated by both. Let's face it, everyone on your team is keenly aware of who the weak performers are, just as they know, without a doubt, who the top performers are. There is nothing confusing about any of that. *What they also know is that if you, as a leader, are allowing the underperformers to continue, then you really do not believe in creating a culture of high performance.* Perhaps you are more interested in protecting your favorites. Or maybe you are not able to have difficult conversations. At the same time, if you are not rewarding and celebrating your top performers, you are sending them and everyone else in your organization a very strong message about what you value—and what you do not.

Together, accountability and recognition form the foundation for a culture where trust, compassion, and success abound. That is why I believe in full visibility. Sharing information creates trust. Then, the better informed everyone is, the easier it is to understand the rationale behind your decisions.

Meanwhile, there is always time to pause and celebrate someone's success. You are looking for that combination of holding everyone accountable to your clear expectations, while also recognizing and rewarding everyone who exceeds those expectations. That is how you connect your head with your heart and create a culture of success.

Your success as a leader starts with a compelling purpose and a clear road map. Knowing where you are going and how you will get there, you can then surround yourself with the right people—those who can build a winning, sustainable revenue-generation formula, improve your margins, and optimize your operations. In an environment of trust, openness, and collaboration, you can then create continuous accountability, reward those who exceed expectations, celebrate your wins, refine your strategy, and continue to identify and develop the talent within your organization.

SPEND TIME WITH YOUR TOP PERFORMERS

I want to emphasize that connecting your purpose, strategy, and people is an ongoing and continuous process. As a key part of that process, I encourage you to leave your office. Get out and spend valuable time with your top performers. Become familiar with people in your organization who have enormous potential. What do they see that is working extremely well? And what would they like to fix? Visit your newest and your most important clients, too, and learn what they are most enthused and most concerned about. Ask everyone you come across what they are feeling positive about. Then be open to their advice. *What do they believe is the most important thing you should be focusing on?* Get in touch with any clients you may have lost to see how they are doing and if there is a new way you could help them. Ask questions. And be open. Constantly. Always be seeking to discover whether your direction needs to be adjusted. Is your strategy on course? Do you have the right people in the right places? Are you missing something? Anything? Could your organization quickly respond to an unexpected change in the marketplace?

You want to look broadly outside your organization, as well as deeply within.

Keep asking questions. And test the answers.

That is how you will lead by connecting your head with your heart, applying and constantly fine-tuning the connections among your purpose, strategy, and people.

WHEN MAKING STRATEGIC DECISIONS

As a leader, when it comes to making decisions, you can be inundated with advice. Objective and subjective information can come from colleagues, clients, advisors, experts, industry publications, and countless sources interested in affecting your decision. Take it all in. Consider the source. Then there comes a time when you need to stop gathering information. You have to filter out what is important, discard what is not, and make your decision.

Whether you are deciding to adjust your approach to the marketplace or to move someone into a key position—whatever the choice, it is yours. This is when your true leadership kicks into high gear.

You will face major decisions, which, you may realize at the time, are a test of your true leadership ability. That can be overwhelming. What if you are wrong? How could a mistake affect your career? I understand how making such important decisions can cause you to pause. I have seen leaders abdicate or hold off on making a major decision until time made it for them. To me, that is not leading.

When you have enough information, make the decision. The organization knows the situation. They are looking for you to decide. Which way are you going? Anyone can postpone a decision. But indecisiveness only prolongs the agony. It kills purpose, strategy, and engagement. And destroys companies.

Leading is about deciding, then acting on your decisions with integrity, and sharing your reasons with clarity.

This takes believing in yourself. Most of the time, you are going to make the right decision. So, believe it.

Sometimes, you will fail. But if you do not make decisions, you will surely fail.

When you are wrong, take responsibility. Then make an even better decision about how to correct your mistake. When you are right, give credit to everyone in the organization. And carry on.

Let's consider a difficult strategic decision you might have to make. Let's say that the economy has turned, and you need to cut expenses by 10 percent. After making operational adjustments, it becomes clear that you have no choice but to let some people go. What do you consider when making those painful decisions about who stays and who leaves? If you decide that it is only fair to make the cuts unilaterally and ask the leader of every department to eliminate 10 percent of his or her team, you are not leading. While that might sound "fair," such a decision is not leading with your head *or* your heart. As a leader, you want to make those decisions strategically with insight into the marketplace and a clear understanding of where those cuts will incur the least damage to your organization's future. Making such decisions is where you prove your value as a leader.

For me, the more difficult a situation becomes, the quieter my mind becomes—to the point where all other background sounds disappear, and I can focus with clarity on only those things where I can make a significant difference. I am seeking a strategic path. That is where my complete attention goes. I need to find the answer to one question: What can we do most quickly that will have the biggest impact on implementing our strategy? If our strategy is focused on five goals, that does not mean that I necessarily need to let up on those goals. I just need to adjust my emphasis to those priorities where we can have the most immediate impact. Then, after listening to advice, and considering our options, I make my best-informed decision and let everyone know the rationale behind why we are adjusting our direction.

The last thing in the world an organization needs is for decisions to get pocket vetoed or held up in some committee. That is when momentum is lost and people begin to lose faith.

As a leader, you earn your stripes by the decisions you make.

So long as you are transparent about your underlying reasons, and your decisions clearly connect with your purpose and strategy, people will know that the organization is moving forward.

Again, it all comes back to trust. When trust exists in a culture, then a problem is just something to be solved—sooner, rather than later.

CREATING A PURPOSE AND STRATEGY THAT CONNECTS WITH YOUR TEAM: QUESTIONS FOR SELF-EVALUATION

The questions we ask ourselves, and how deeply we answer them, help to shape who we become. With that in mind, I encourage you to dive deeply as you explore these questions. Then review your answers from time to time. And allow your answers to evolve. Your answers will serve as road signs on your leadership journey.

1. What is your organization's purpose?
2. What is your strategy for winning?
3. When was the last time you conducted a full strategic review?
4. Does the marketplace agree that your strategy is worth investing in?
5. What is the key distinction between you and your competitors? How quickly could they make that distinction disappear?
6. Do you have the right people in the right positions to make your strategy succeed?
7. Do the descriptions of your key jobs reflect your strategy? (Or are you just moving the people you have into places where they might fit?)
8. Have you created a common goal for your team to connect with?
9. Do you have transparent metrics that are published for everyone to see?

10. Do you reward and recognize performance?
11. Do you hold everyone accountable—including those who are not performing up to expectations?
12. Do you hold yourself accountable?
13. Do you recognize and reward those who are exceeding expectations?
14. How do you make important decisions?

CHAPTER 9

CONNECTING WITH THE HEARTS OF YOUR CUSTOMERS

When you have strong, genuine connections inside your organization—relationships between colleagues where there is trust, openness, and compassion—they can then permeate to the outside—to your clients, business partners, and prospects, who will know that the warmth they are feeling is real. Because it comes from the inside out. Likewise, business relationships are not arm's-length associations. At their very best, they can become as deep as they are wide.

With that belief, one of my goals was to have the compassion we were feeling for each other within our organization spread from all of us to our customers. With this newfound resurgence, I believed, would come market share growth, margin improvement, and a huge turnaround in shareholder value.

That is why, when I became Avis Budget Group's president for North America, I set out to meet each of our major business partners. One of my first stops was to see Dave Ridley, senior vice president and chief marketing officer of Southwest Airlines. As I sat in his office, I could not help but notice several impressive souvenirs from some of the renowned golf courses where he has played. He was clearly a huge golf fan—or, as Dave says, "a fanatic."

Being naturally curious, I asked him about some of his favorite golf courses. He told me about the more memorable places he had played. Then, I suppose since Avis Budget Group's headquarters is in New Jersey, he asked if I had ever played at Pine Valley, and I said I hadn't. His eyes lit up and he said, "That's on my bucket list. Right at the top."

So, I just smiled, and jotted a note to myself. Then after the meeting, I called Norb Gambuzza, who is now the senior vice president of corporate affairs for the PGA Tour, was a business partner, and remains a close friend. I asked him if he knew anyone who was a member of Pine Valley. Norb came through, as he always does, which enabled us to play at Pine Valley, and let Dave tick off something major from his bucket list. It also created an opportunity for me to get to know Dave much better. I gleaned insights into what motivates him, his interests, his family, what Southwest was like when he started there in the late eighties, and, most importantly, how our values were aligned. From there, we were able to see a way for both of us to build what was a $40 million relationship into one worth over $100 million—one that benefitted all of us, including, ultimately, our customers.

Dave shared, "When Tom came on, he was putting his people first, believing the feeling would permeate, as they would put their customers first. And it was working. During those first years when I met him, I could tell the difference whenever I went up to an Avis counter. He set the stage, encouraging everyone around him to show who they were at their very best, and you could feel the result reflected in the culture of the organization."

He further recalled, "Tom has a way of finding a genuine connection with whoever he is talking to. I have seen him engage with people. And he is entirely there. People really appreciate that and respond to it. He builds trust by being open about who he is and by caring about you. And by being true to his emotions. He looks for that connection, wherever it is. You can try to train for that all you want, but if it does not come from the heart, it is not real." As a result, he added, "My relationship with Tom was not like a business relationship that evolved into a personal relationship. It started out as both. Instantly. It is the most unique blend of both, and that is very rare in the world of business."

My firm belief is that finding "the personal" in your relationships is key to succeeding in business. It's true whether those relationships are with the people you are working with or with your customers (the customers I'll address specially in this chapter are business partners). The deeper you connect with someone, the more compassion you show them, the more you and they will thrive. That is why my advice is to allow the personal and professional to blend. There is no need to create any difference between those two worlds.

The connection Dave and I have transcends the typical bounds of a business relationship—enriching both of our lives in ways that are still unfolding. Just by way of a quick example, while I am no longer at Avis, Dave recently lent my family his house to stay in while our daughter was in the hospital with her prematurely born son. When your connections are deep, boundaries disappear, and your life becomes richer in ways that can constantly amaze you.

CONNECTING PEOPLE WITH IDEAS TO CREATE POSSIBILITIES

When I joined Avis, one of my personal goals, in addition to meeting with our key clients and forming closer relationships with them, was to elevate our brand as a premier provider of automobiles. I wanted to catapult the Avis brand to a new level, so people would start to think differently about who we were. This is where connecting people you know with ideas you share can create new possibilities for each of you. *The closer you are and the more you know about your clients (and they know about you), the more opportunities arise. It all starts with your connections.*

When I first met Adam Johnson, chairman and CEO of NetJets, a subsidiary of Berkshire Hathaway, I was fascinated to learn more about him personally and professionally. Flying, he told me, "has always been in my blood." Both his grandfathers were aircraft mechanics. His dad worked at GE Aircraft Engines. And, as he said, he "just always wanted to be in and around flying in some capacity." He took his first ultralight flying lesson when he was thirteen, describing it as having "a snowmobile engine and a kite wing." That was when he got "the fever." He started flying when he was eighteen, then went to Ohio State for the flight program, which I know to be one of the best in the country. He was flying small single-engine private aircraft there and loved being in the air. But by the time he graduated, he realized he had become more intrigued by the business of flying.

I love learning what draws someone to their passion. My "lesson" starts with a natural curiosity, then just asking questions and being truly interested. In addition to often being fascinating, such conversations help to broaden my understanding of who someone is, and thus deepen our relationship.

Fast-forward in Adam's career to where he is now at the helm of NetJets, which operates in a rarified world, selling fractional ownership of private business jets to the wealthiest one-tenth of 1 percent of the world's population.

As Adam described, "NetJets had been using Avis to transport a lot of our owners, so our partnership is important. The total value in our program is judged on the entire experience we provide—from getting our owners to their plane to the flight itself to getting them to their destination after the flight. Every aspect of that experience is expected to be perfect."

As I sought to elevate our brand as a premier provider of automobiles, our partnership with NetJets was clearly a very important place to focus. First and foremost, I needed to make sure that we were providing the white-glove service that NetJets owners expected. In our first conversation, Adam and I explored, openly and honestly, how Avis could improve our service to ensure we were exceeding his expectations. I assured him that nothing would fall through the cracks. Then I worked with our team to establish surefire procedures for delivering superior service. Adam shared, "As Tom and I worked together, I saw him change his organization's culture, motivating people to provide the best service in the world."

Then, as our relationship grew, I asked Adam if he would help me create a partnership with Mercedes-Benz. I added, "Mercedes would be a perfect client for NetJets, as well."

Then I confided, "We want to upgrade. And we have wanted to create an agreement with Mercedes for a long time. But we have had some challenges. They have not been willing to commit vehicles to us along the way." Pausing, I added, "Mercedes exemplifies your brand, and it exemplifies the brand that we want to be known as."

Then we talked about how we might make this happen together. And we did.

What was that meeting like? Adam described it: "It was with some of the key executives from Mercedes, who were sitting around a table with Tom and me. And Tom masterfully described the dream, getting everyone enthused, then engaged in making it happen."

I assured them that I understood completely that Mercedes, like NetJets, is a very sophisticated luxury brand that is naturally cautious about who it partners with. Then I started sharing with them why it made sense for all three of our companies to work together. While I knew that initially it might appear as a leap of faith for Mercedes, I portrayed how a NetJets owner driving off in a Mercedes rented from Avis would be the end of a perfect day.

As Adam described, "Tom very convincingly brought everyone along for the ride and guided the meeting to make sure the Mercedes executives saw that partnering with Net-Jets and Avis was exactly what they needed to do, and how it would enhance the Mercedes brand—which, of course, is one of the most recognized symbols of luxury in the world."

Adam added, "Tom knows where he wants to go. Then he builds the story so that people feel they are part of it and want to collaborate. It is a true talent. Many senior exec-utives will say, 'Here's what we need to do. So, let's do it.' Tom, instead, brings you along for the journey. He under-stands how we can all be in it together. He is able to build an unusual level of trust with the people around him, culti-vating friendships in his business colleagues and partners. And, as a result, he creates friends. He also makes it fun. He is a very tough businessman. But he makes you want to be on the journey with him."

Taking people on the journey with you. That is what you do as a leader when you truly connect with others.

PERSONAL RELATIONSHIPS TRANSCEND BOUNDARIES

Another key partner that was important for me to connect with when I began at Avis was Priceline.com, which, of course, is renowned for providing deep discounts on hotels, flights, and rental cars. Now, I knew from their business model that the hotel business is at the center of Priceline's bookings. That is where there are healthy margins, though the market is very fragmented. The airline industry, meanwhile, has become more of an oligopoly. So, for instance, at Dallas–Fort Worth, American Airlines has cornered that market, since that is their largest hub. The rental car business, on the other hand, focuses on the three major companies—Avis, Hertz, and Enterprise—which, compared to hotels and airlines, comprise a relatively small portion of Priceline's profits.

Still, I knew that there might be ways to work more closely that would benefit both of our organizations. Fortunately, when I met with Chris Soder, former CEO and president of Priceline.com, he and I connected immediately. As Chris described, "A personal relationship with Tom quickly evolved, based on our common values."

He paused, then added, "I have come across many people in this business for whom integrity doesn't appear to be a priority. Fortunately, I have a pretty good sense for when someone is genuine. So, that creates a whole different working relationship, with different rules and guidelines. When you can be completely open in a negotiation, you can focus solely on creating the best business deal.

"For Tom and me, from the beginning, there was a deep level of trust. If we had a verbal agreement, that was all we needed. Afterward, we would cross the *t*'s and dot the *i*'s. But in reaching the deal, we did not have to worry about those things. Because we believed in each other implicitly. From my perspective, Tom is at the top of the pyramid of business relationships that begin with trust and honesty and become personal, as a result."

By understanding Priceline.com's business model, and asking Chris questions about what he needed to succeed, I was able to collaborate with him to create ways for both of our organizations to profit. Just by way of example, we placed our family discount business solely with Priceline.com, and they returned a higher rate of business for us. Over the time we had that arrangement, Chris said, "it created significant value for Avis, while helping Priceline become the fastest-growing online rental car provider. Our business experienced significant growth at a time when the other key players were basically flat. Part of the driver of that success was the preferred arrangement that we had with Avis. Priceline.com received better supply, Avis had better distribution, and both sides grew significantly as a result."

One of the things that occurred when Chris and I became close was that we went on a hunting trip to Argentina. As he explained, "That trip came out of a golf tournament I attended with Tom. During the tournament, our group was having a great time. When the auction came to the end, the last item was a hunting trip to Argentina, which was hosted by Craig Stadler (the Walrus), the 1982 Masters Champion. And there were four of us having a lot of fun together, and we agreed, whatever it costs, we were going to win that trip. And we did. But then one of the guys had to pull out. So, I immediately thought, I'd like to bring my dad along on this trip—since I grew up hunting with him."

It was an amazing experience, which, of course, we all paid for personally. Toward the end of the trip, we were in a hunting lodge, sharing some wine and memories, and I asked Chris's dad, "How long have you and your wife been married?" And his dad opened up, telling some very touching stories about how he and his wife first met, and the experiences they shared together. And I could tell it was cathartic for him, and meaningful for all of us.

Chris said, "Tom could not have been more supportive or nicer to my dad. And that endeared him to me forever because of the way he connected with my dad. Tom also got emotional and shared about how great it was to spend time with my dad because he had lost his father when he was a teenager. And it was just so powerful. It touched me on a personal level. And my dad still asks about Tom to this day. He keeps reminding me, 'Tom is a good man.' So, in a hunting lodge, with a couple of other guys, my dad and Tom both broke down and shared their emotions. That is very rare. And it mattered a lot to my dad. It was quite amazing."

Chris added, "Most guys get the message along the way to check your emotions. Tom, though, is able to blend his personal and professional life seamlessly—more beautifully than anyone I know."

LOOK FOR THE CONNECTION

Allow me to include one more story about how connecting on a deep level in a professional relationship led to a friendship that means the world to me.

Norb Gambuzza, senior vice president of corporate affairs for the PGA Tour, and I got to know each other very well when we were negotiating a deal that became valuable for both of our organizations. As he said, "We all have business relationships that become personal, as well. But with Tom, that occurs on a very profound level."

He explained, "After he and I struck the deal, Ellen, my wife, and I took Tom and Barb out to dinner to celebrate. That's when we started to develop this extremely meaningful connection. Then they came over to our house and met our kids, and it all just seemed very natural. 'Family First' is Tom's guiding principle. And I am sure he recognized how vitally important my family is in my life, as well. For me, work is important, but my family comes first."

Norb added, "Our sons Michael and Charlie are teenagers. And we taught them that when you meet someone who is older, you shake their hand and say, 'Hello, Mr. Gartland.' And I know he just got them. When he and Barb bought a house near us in Florida, he started teaching my children. He would have them take care of his plants or wash his car and pay them for their chores. Then, he also took time to talk with them about what was going on in their lives. He has become like a surrogate uncle to my children. He is as interested in them as they are in him. He tells them stories about how he started out with nothing. And teaches them about the importance of having a solid work ethic. He does not just say this stuff. Tom lives it—to the benefit of my children."

One of my guiding principles is that *if you truly connect with someone whose values you respect—whether personally or professionally—then open up and let each other in.* Finding "the personal" in your relationships is the key to succeeding in business, to bringing people on the journey with you, and, along the way, to enriching their lives as well as yours.

In much the same way, you can truly connect with your business partners through sharing yourself and genuinely caring about them. It means creating the opportunity to spend quality, one-on-one time together; understanding their personal value system; getting to know what is important in their lives as well as within their companies; and creating ways to drive the strength of your relationship, along with incremental revenue that is enduring and in the best interest of both of your companies.

When you connect with a business partner or customer, open yourself up to the possibility that your relationship can enhance both of your lives. Do not look for the sale. Look for the connection. Engage. Be there entirely. That is how you will stand out from the crowd. Those you want to connect with will appreciate your being interested in them. Let them know that you care—for them, for their organization, and for new possibilities.

Be open to becoming partners with them. And allow the relationship to evolve. What is the worst thing that can happen? You may be surprised by the best thing that happens.

Whether the relationships you develop are with the people you are working with, your customers, your neighbors, your friends, or your family, the more deeply you connect with them, the more trust and love you show each other, the more you and they will thrive.

GOLF IS THE ULTIMATE GAME FOR DEVELOPING RELATIONSHIPS

When Barb and I first married, I was twenty years old and still going to the College of St. Thomas (now a university). When we found out that she was expecting our daughter Sara, I got a job at a steel fabricating plant during the day, while finishing school at night. I worked on a plate shear, where a 10-by-20-foot, half-inch-thick sheet of steel would roll up in front of me, and I would cut it to specifications. Then a huge magnet would sweep down, pick it up, and stack it on top of the others I had just cut.

As soon as each of my fifteen-minute breaks came around, I would rush outside to smoke a cigarette and gaze across the way at Midland Hills Country Club, thinking, "I've got to get a job like that—where I can take customers out to play golf."

It took a while for me to get my own set of golf clubs and realize why I was so drawn to the game. I soon realized that golf can be *much* more than the escape I was originally seeking. Golf, it turns out, is a game of integrity, honor, and ethics. It is also a way to get to know yourself as well as someone else on a much deeper level.

As Steve Stricker, who has won twelve PGA Tour events in his career, shared with me, "Golf is a mirror image of your life. The game can teach you a lot about yourself—as well as whoever you are playing with. From someone's tempo on the course, you can tell a lot about who they are. When things are not going your way, how do you react? How are you when things are going better than you could possibly hope for? Can you keep the same demeanor depending upon which way things are going? Whatever the answer, the chances are, you will be the same way on the course as you are in the rest of your life. At the end of the day, I believe you swing at the ball the way you swing at life."

I thrived on team sports when I was in high school and college, where I learned an enormous amount about discipline, confidence, trust, relationships, losing, and winning. But there really is no other game like golf for developing relationships. Where else can you get one-on-one time with someone for several hours? When you get on the golf course, there are no cell phones, there are no interruptions. (How unusual is that in this world?) You are just outside in a beautiful place. And as you are playing, connections occur, and, sometimes, real camaraderie.

One of the most interesting things about golf, for me, is that while you are always just playing the game against yourself, it is still a perfect game for building relationships. And, as Steve said, you can quickly discover a lot about what someone else is made of when you are playing with them. Are they competitive by nature? If so, how do they compete? Do they follow the rules of the game? How do they react when things are not going their way? And how gracious are they when they win? Do they know how to win like a champion? And lose like a champion? How will they deal with difficult situations? Do they count their strokes? Do they take it all too personally? You can find out a lot about a person's demeanor and integrity when you play golf together. And it is a much more open and honest place than just having lunch with someone, where they can present themselves a certain way for a short period of time.

Meanwhile, what golf also provides is an unusual amount of time to connect with and get to really know someone—on a personal and professional level. Particularly in our fast-paced world, it can often be difficult just to get on someone's schedule for an hour in any business setting. And to carve out several hours is almost impossible. Golf, then, becomes the perfect opportunity for developing and deepening relationships.

From hole to hole and shot to shot, you can realize a lot about someone—just by asking questions, being curious, and truly caring. As you are engaged in something that you both enjoy, in a place you love to be, the conversation becomes easy. What matters to them? And what does not? What are their values? Their hobbies? Their worries? How are things going for them? What do they really care about? Or worry about? Is there some way, any way, you might be able to help them?

Golf is really about a shared experience, and the beautiful background of wherever you are playing informs your conversation. Every golf course is gorgeous, yet different. And some of the courses are *very* special, among the most beautiful places on the planet. So, if you are there, outside, in that majestic beauty, something about that experience will stay with both of you forever. Add to that, every golfer has his or her own bucket list, whether it is Pebble

Beach, Pine Valley, St. Andrews, Augusta, Pinehurst, Royal County Down, Cypress Point, the TPC Stadium Course, or any of the other top places to play in the world. To be fortunate enough to play on such courses with someone creates a memory that lasts forever.

There is little wonder why Dave Ridley, the former chief marketing officer of Southwest Airlines, whom I developed a deep relationship with after our first golf outing, describes the game this way: "Golf feeds my soul unlike any activity other than worshipping in church. I love everything about the game: the setting, the challenge, the competition, the companionship, and the keen insights it provides into people."

For developing relationships, golf is the best game I know. And you can play it on many levels.

CONNECTING WITH THE HEARTS OF YOUR CUSTOMERS: QUESTIONS FOR SELF-EVALUATION

The questions we ask ourselves, and how deeply we answer them, help to shape who we become. With that in mind, I encourage you to dive deeply as you explore these questions. Then review your answers from time to time. And allow your answers to evolve. Your answers will serve as road signs on your leadership journey.

1. How would you describe your ability to build relationships?
2. What is one thing you could do to connect more deeply with people? When will you practice it? With whom?
3. What can you do to put yourself in the shoes of each of your customers?
4. What questions could you ask to get to know them better?
5. How can you show them that you care about them?
6. What is the shared passion you have with each of your customers? (Children? Sports? Traveling? Music?)
7. What could you do with each of them to connect on a deeper level?
8. What about them—or their business—fascinates you?

9. What values do you share?
10. How do you focus on each of them? Do you focus on what you want? Or on what they need?
11. How can you make each of your customers look like a hero within their organization?
12. Do you look for opportunities to make each of them part of your work family?
13. Do you stay in touch over time (not just when an opportunity arises)? Do you find real reasons to stay in touch? (This is a measure of the authenticity of your relationship.)

CHAPTER 10

SEEING NEW POSSIBILITIES
WITH YOUR COACH

L eading is not a solo mission. You cannot do it alone. No one can. In fact, leading with your heart requires acknowledging that you need, and welcome, help—so that you can continue helping others. Otherwise, your well will run dry.

Where can you find such help?

When I am struggling with a difficult situation, I often reflect upon the advice I received from two of my mentors.

First, there is Jack Lachenmayer, who hired me as a salesperson for Ecolab after I graduated from college. We have remained friends throughout our lives. In fact, I was grateful to return the favor just a few years ago when I had the opportunity to hire him to help develop our corporate accounts representatives at Avis Budget Group. Everything about Jack, even his smallest expressions, conveys trust.

When I first started at Ecolab, I realized, just by watching him connect with his customers or with his team, why I, too, was putting my hand over my heart whenever I wanted to make a point that I felt deeply. Some things we learn through osmosis. I also carry with me something he may not even remember saying, which was, "Tom, at the end of each day, all that matters is that when I go home at night, I can look myself in the mirror and say that I gave it my best shot. Was I true to my values, to my family, and to my company? And did I do everything I could to be successful?"

I also think back to Jim McCarty, who taught me more than anyone else in my career. He was a true mentor and the best boss I ever had. He went on to become the senior executive vice president for the Institutional Group at Ecolab. When I became a manager there, I used to stop by his office at six o'clock in the morning and bring him a cup of coffee. Then I would bombard him with questions and seek his advice about what I needed to do to keep improving. As with most great teachers, he taught me as much by what he did as by what he said. Just by way of a quick example, before I took on a new management position, Barb and I were very excited to vacation in the Cayman Islands. When we got to our hotel room, there was a bottle of Dom Pérignon waiting for us, with a note from Jim that read, "Have a great vacation!" That was it. He was saying, "Take time for yourself. And enjoy!" That just blew me away! After that, I would have done anything for that guy. He was also an inspiring orator. And he was always writing notes to people, letting them know what a great job they were doing. He taught me an enormous amount about how to lead by truly caring for those around us. And to let them know.

EVERY LEADER NEEDS A COACH

Your mentors can show you the ropes and provide advice as they become your role models. They can also be the source of memories that inform your personal and professional credo. As you proceed on your leadership journey, *reaching out and connecting with your mentors can remind you of who you are at your very best.*

But there will also be times when you find that *you need a new perspective.*

For instance, you may be considering a challenging organizational decision. Or perhaps you are having a personality conflict with another leader in your organization. Or there might be something inside yourself that you realize is holding you back from your next career move.

How can you make sure that you are thoroughly considering every possible option?

Left within the confines of your own office, it is difficult to get outside of your own frame of mind to create new options. While your colleagues can help brainstorm ideas, you all may be limited by your organizational perspective. You can certainly find enormous support from your loved ones, but naturally it will be difficult for them to remain objective.

To keep honing your leadership gifts, there are times when you need to talk in complete confidence with someone with executive experience who can provide you with an external, completely objective perspective. Ideally, this person will become a sounding board who is also able to ask questions that cause you to pause. This person will support you as you explore new options, while occasionally offering unvarnished advice that you need to hear.

Admittedly, that is a tall order to fill.

That is why I firmly believe that every leader needs a coach.

A coach can help you to candidly explore your concerns, doubts, blind spots, aspirations, and dreams—while helping you stay focused on what is most important for your organization as well as your personal growth.

For me, that coach has been Tim Stratman. As a former leader at Fortune 500 companies, he knows the pressure-cooker environment. He also brings a unique blend of supporting and challenging me, which has often caught me off guard at just the right moment. While he certainly encourages my aspirations, Tim is also able to test my assumptions with empowering questions that can cause me to reconsider the thoughts or feelings I am having—or something I am about to do. Some of his questions, asked at just the right time, can be as simple, yet important, as *What is another way to look at this? How will you feel if this happens? How does this decision confirm your values?*

THE COACHING RELATIONSHIP

A successful coaching arrangement requires chemistry between you and your coach, along with a deep level of trust, openness, honesty, self-awareness, and an unwavering motivation on your part to keep improving.

When you are considering a coach, the chemistry between the two of you is of the utmost importance. Does your coach "get" you? Is it easy (but not too easy) to talk with him or her? Can your coach question you in such a way that it feels like you are challenging yourself like you never have before?

While coaching is a completely confidential process, with Tim's permission, and without betraying any confidences, I will share with you some candid stories and insights into our coaching relationship. My hope in being so transparent is that it might help you to understand that there may be ways in which you, too, at times, may not be coming across as you intend. Then, with self-awareness, a hunger to improve, and the help of a coach, you will be able to turn those situations around—to become an even better leader.

When I first came to Avis, I was most interested in working with a coach because I was starting out in a new environment, I was in a different part of the country, and, in many ways, I felt like I was beginning a new chapter of my life.

From my initial hiring interviews, it was clear to me that this organization was full of extremely bright people who had a very strong analytical and operationally based perspective. One of my key strengths, on the other hand, is my ability and desire to connect with people, to put them first.

When I arrived on my first day, I wanted to make an immediate impact, as was my nature. But I was also keenly aware that many organizations can be prone to "organ rejection," which is code for *when a new leader appears from the outside with a different style or approach, people can make a quick decision that he or she "is not one of us."*

So, being an unknown agent of change, I did not want to be blindsided by any resistance within the organization. That is a large part of the reason why I was initially motivated to connect with an executive coach. I needed to quickly glean purely objective feedback (very difficult to get inside of any organization) about how I was connecting with my new peers, as well as everyone on my team and members of the board. I also needed to know if there were any roadblocks within the organization or shortcomings within myself that I might not be aware of. And I was intent on continuing to improve as a leader, while honoring my core values.

As my coach Tim said, "It was clear that Tom represented a different viewpoint and perspective. So, one of the questions was: *Could he make his style not only work for him but accelerate results in a culture that was very different?* Tom's approach and style—being extroverted, open, passionate, and focused on people—were completely different from what people in the organization were used to or expected."

Our conversations focused on how I could successfully navigate these new waters, while being true to myself.

From a coach's point of view, Tim explained, "Tom can be seen as a flashy guy. He has a presence. He can control the room. He is outgoing and outspoken. So, when he first got to Avis, I coached him around subordinating his emotional responses. If he heard something that seemed completely outrageous or just did not make sense, I cautioned him, when you are new, you have to address those things carefully. You need to develop relationships that can support your challenges. Otherwise, people will just shut down. Sometimes, when you are new to the scene, you have to bite your tongue and wait for the best time to address a particular situation. A lot of this was around adapting his style. Sometimes it was just about small things. Mostly, it was letting people know that he got them."

In the beginning, I had to consider, then reconsider, some of the feedback and advice that Tim provided me. One of the things I needed to come to terms with and accept was the realization that, being new, I was inadvertently ruffling some people's feathers.

To provide a backdrop for what was happening at the time, Barbara Kogen, who was vice president of organizational development and performance, explained, "When Tom first started, his position had been open for more than a year. And he came on with a very strong presence. So, a lot of people were taken aback and feeling unsure about this new guy. You could tell that was not the reaction he was seeking. But there were quite a few people who were intimidated because they were not used to being in the presence of such passionate energy."

Tom Villani, whom I promoted several times from originally being a pricing manager to vice president of global travel and partnerships, concurred that a lot of people were actually frightened of me when I started. "He made it clear that he was all about getting the right talent in the right roles," he explained. "And it did not take long for him to assess what was going on, then start making some very strong moves. That scared a lot of people (mostly those who needed to be scared). But for those of us who wanted to succeed, it made the place very exciting."

You realize, when you enter a new situation as a leader, that *some people are rooting for you to make quick positive changes; others are taking a wait-and-see approach.* Then there are those who are resistant because they do not understand why you are in this new position, rather than them. So, the dynamics can get complicated, which is why the insights from a coach can provide you with a much-needed objective perspective.

Tim explained, "I shared a lot of feedback with Tom about how he was not coming across to a few people on the leadership team as he intended. To his credit, he was able to negotiate that subtly. He understood how to adapt his style enough so that he started connecting more effectively with those individuals, while still being true to himself." He added, "His ability to take all of that in, and not be defensive, was admirable."

In the beginning, through our conversations, Tim helped me become more aware of situations I otherwise might have missed. Then, with that understanding and perspective, I reflected on how I was going to turn the situation around with people who, I realized, were simply seeing things differently than I was.

For instance, there was one area that I had to overcome that made absolutely no sense to me. But, as they say, perception can become reality. So, you have to be careful whenever you hear a warning sign.

Let me allow Tim to explain: "Tom can fill a room with his energy. But like any strength, it can have a downside. Early on, there was a perception by a few members of the leadership team that, since Tom was not a finance guy, he did not understand the P&L."

He added, "Now, of course, Tom knew finances inside and out. He had already been the president of JohnsonDiversey. He had spoken with investors and board members with great ease about intricate financial projections. But a few people in the organization were coming from a preconceived notion that if you are outgoing and focused on creating relationships, then your success is all about smiles and connections. So, I coached Tom on being patient and on strategically demonstrating his analytical and strategic skills."

Tim's guidance was very helpful as I shifted through these perceptions and eased into letting people know that I was actually much better at analyzing financials than they might have realized. Quite frankly, I found it difficult to believe that I had to prove this. But I bit my tongue and said, "Okay. I'll take these steps."

It is troublesome knowing that someone does not think you get something that you do. Then it is doubly hard to go through a process where you have to prove something that you already know. But, before our next few important meetings, I made a point of having individual conversations with certain people to validate my understanding of our financial situation and to appreciate their perspective. Then, during the meetings, I would just make a pointed observation about our P&L. And my financial acumen quickly became a nonissue. Tim's coaching was helpful in my being able to overcome the perceptions and just let it go. *It was about becoming more self-aware, recognizing when my buttons were being pushed, and considering how I was going to respond, rather than just react.*

There were also situations where Tim coached me on being patient with people who were hesitant to act. In my case, once I have considered enough information and I am ready to act, I want to pull the trigger. If the evidence is pointing in a clear direction, then why in the world would we wait? But through Tim's coaching, I came to realize that there are some people whom I need to allow more time for, so they can take in and sort through the information, then come to their own conclusions. In such situations, my tendency is to want to make things happen quickly. So, I learned that, outside of an emergency, having more than one speed is a definite asset. I became fine with that, so long as we kept moving in the right direction.

Sometimes I would also call Tim and say, "I just want to run something by you." It could have been when I was just coming out of a meeting and something was fresh in my mind. Often, in those situations, in the moment, that is where the most immediate and valuable coaching can occur.

Still, throughout it all, Tim's underlying coaching philosophy was consistent: *I needed to focus on being my authentic self, while bringing others along with me.*

When I moved from being the head of sales, marketing, and customer care to Avis Budget Group's president for North America, I also looked to Tim to help me navigate some of those significant changes.

A specific example of that came when I decided to initiate The Bus Tour. As Tim recalled, "Tom and his team were going to stop at virtually every location within North America and let all twenty thousand people know how vitally important each and every one of them was to the organization's success. That was his idea. And it was big. But it was not, by any stretch of the imagination, immediately understood as a priority by several members of the leadership team. Some of them were saying to each other, 'Wait a minute. You're going to rent a bus? And you're going to take the bus for several months and press the flesh with everyone in every location? And just how in the world is that going to pay off?' "

Tim helped me step back and consider why several people on the leadership team were not as enthused about this idea as I was. Catching my breath, I took it all in. Then, later that day, at the weekly leadership meeting, I looked everyone in the eye and said, "I realize that not everyone recognizes the value of what we are about to do. I understand that. But I am asking you to trust me on this. This will be a game changer for our company. I promise you."

Then I paused, and added, "I get that we are in a commodity business. You go to an airport, and you can rent a car from a lot of different vendors, so we need to manage costs and price extremely well to show a profit. That will always be important. But, at the end of the day, our people are what differentiates us. That feeling that we are all in it together and care deeply about what we are doing—that is what separates us from our competition. That is why we need to show our employees how very important they are, and how much we truly care. This can be the lynchpin for the future success of our company.

"Meanwhile, I assure you, our business will carry on as usual. The bus has Wi-Fi, so we will be in constant touch with our teams, and we won't miss a beat on our day-to-day management activities. Most importantly, the connections we make with our employees will create an entirely new level of engagement. And our customers will feel it. The payback will be astounding, I assure you. When we focus on people, the profits will follow."

Heads were nodding as I spoke. And some of those nods were the ones I was looking for. Then, after the meeting, I made a point of getting together individually with everyone on the leadership team, including the nonbelievers, and asking for their advice on how we could make this effort even more effective. Then I made sure that everyone was informed about every step of the planning and execution of The Bus Tour. That is also why I decided to bring some of our most committed and engaged employees back to head-quarters on the last day of the tour. Once everyone at our corporate headquarters saw and felt the connections we had made, they forgot all doubt.

Tim underscored, "The executives that coaches work with are constantly striving to get better. And the higher they go in the organization, the harder that becomes." He added, "As a coach, you are not there as a friend. You can certainly be friends. But you need to remain objective and above the fray. The value you bring is in helping leaders identify and see patterns in themselves that they might not otherwise. Then to see new possibilities for themselves and others. I do this by listening, asking a lot of questions, and occasionally providing insights or a perspective. *The goal is always the same: to help a leader understand the situation in a new way. And to realize that there are more options available than they initially realized.*"

As it turns out, most of us are in leadership positions because we have an enormous amount of confidence and assertiveness. So, we are, by nature, action oriented. But, as Tim noted, too much of a good thing is not a good thing. That is where a coach can sometimes help to pull us back from our natural inclination to do something, anything. The questions a coach asks can help us to pause and reflect on all the options available to us—and then create even more options.

THE RESULTS FROM COACHING

Tim's empowering questions have a way of helping me arrive at a clear way of seeing into myself *and* the world around me. He also helps me see patterns that I might not otherwise. Talking through issues with him can help me decide which matters I can give a little on, and which ones I cannot. Most importantly, he helps me create options. There is an enormous value in having more options. A lot of times, as leaders, we may be approaching a decision as though there is only one best choice. Or we can get into thinking that there is a right choice and a wrong choice. And the last thing we want to do is to make the wrong choice. But there are often more options out there, some of which we may not have considered.

While leading is an absolute privilege, the pressures can sometimes be daunting. As leaders, we are responsible for seeing around many corners, responding to market shifts, competitive advances, and financial concerns that can arise before we have our first cup of coffee.

Leaders are defined by our actions, but we also need time for self-reflection and discovery. That is where a coach can help us to get out of our heads and back in touch with our hearts, as we reflect and explore our thoughts and feelings on a deeper level and create new possibilities—for ourselves and our organizations.

THE VALUE OF COACHING CAN BE OVER A HALF-MILLION DOLLARS

I was honored when Steve Stricker, who has been recognized as high as second in the Official World Golf Ranking, agreed to become an ambassador for Avis in 2011. He said, "When I met Tom, we connected on a deep level, very quickly. He is all about family values and having his life in order. And I could see that he brought that same philosophy to his company. So, it felt perfectly natural for me to represent Avis."

Like most professional athletes, Steve has a coach. What is unusual for Steve is that his coach since he was in college has been Dennis Tiziani, who became his father-in-law. Steve said, "From college on, I've continued to learn from Dennis. When I was younger, he would spend two hours a day with me, working on my swing. And I continue to learn from him about my long-iron game as well as my frame of mind."

Interestingly, at the 2013 WGC–Cadillac Championship at Doral, Steve gave Tiger Woods a coaching session on the putting green, which, I teased him, may have cost him over a half-million dollars.

As Steve explained, "While Tiger is one of the best putters in the game, he was struggling to put that part of his game together. We all go through such times." Then, laughing easily and comfortably, he explained, "We ran into each other on the putting green the Wednesday night before the tournament and started talking. Then Tiger asked if I would work with him a little bit, which I was more than glad to do. We practiced for about an hour, and I could see he was catching on to a few things. And his confidence was building."

Tiger ended up winning the tournament, taking the fewest putts over 72 holes in any event. And Steve finished second by two strokes. At the trophy presentation, Tiger, who received over $1.4 million for winning that tournament, gracefully thanked Steve for the putting lesson.

Steve nonchalantly added, "Just like every professional golfer, and I don't think Tiger is any different, you go through a time when you start off and everything seems to be going in your direction. Then you get enough scar tissue from losing some close tournaments. And that starts to wear on your confidence level. And then you seem to hit a certain lull or downtime. That is when you just have to go back and find what was working for you again, and regain your confidence."

That is exactly why the best in every game always have a coach.

In much the same way, Tim Stratman, who has been my coach, shared, "I work with leaders who are already excelling in their careers. They are achievement driven and seeking to compete at the highest level. They often want to be at the helm of the company they are in—or of another company. While being very successful, they are still striving to take one or two strokes off their game. They will freely say, 'I want a coach because I want to keep improving.' That mind-set is what differentiates those who excel."

COACHING LEADERS TO ASK MORE QUESTIONS

To create a positive growth mind-set within your organization, I encourage you and other leaders in your organization to become more like coaches—and ask questions that cause members of your team to pause and consider new options.

This advice might fly in the face of what many leaders believe—that they need to be the source of all answers. While providing answers might seem like the quickest way to make things happen, it is not how learning occurs. Real development occurs when we discover for ourselves the answer to a daunting question. That is when we carry learning with us.

In addition, when leaders ask empowering questions, the ripple effect helps to create a collaborative, encouraging, and engaging culture of constant learning.

How can you and other leaders in your organization begin asking questions that will deepen your decisions and broaden your options?

Let me share a few of the questions that my coach continually challenges me with whenever I have a difficult decision to make. Depending upon the situation, some of the questions might help you—or someone you are coaching:

What is another way to look at this situation? (Then: How can reframing the situation that way help you move forward?)

Which of your key values would you be honoring by
your decision?

What could you be doing differently?

What have you learned from a similar situation?
(Then: How can you apply that to this situation?)

What is draining your energy away from achieving this
goal?

If you had unlimited resources, what would you do in
this situation?

What is the worst thing that could happen?

What is the best thing that could happen?

What do you need to do more of?

What do you need to do less of?

How might you be holding yourself back?

How would trying that feel to you?

How would not trying that feel to you?

What does your heart tell you?

Like most important questions in life, the only answer
that really matters is the one that is true to you.

You want to take your time and consider such
questions—based on the situation you or a colleague is
facing. By compassionately challenging ourselves and
those around us to consider new options—and to dig deep
within—we can create a culture where the questions we
ask help to create new possibilities.

At the end of the day, the right answer to the wrong
question is not as valuable as the right question asked at
just the right time.

SEEING NEW POSSIBILITIES WITH YOUR COACH: QUESTIONS FOR SELF-EVALUATION

The questions we ask ourselves, and how deeply we answer them, help to shape who we become. With that in mind, I encourage you to dive deeply as you explore these questions. Then review your answers from time to time. And allow your answers to evolve. Your answers will serve as road signs on your leadership journey.

1. What do you believe a coach can help you with most? Have you identified what you want to work on?
2. Have you had a 360 review with your team? What were your initial impressions? Your second thoughts?
3. Have you shared with your team the results from your 360 review, along with your perceptions and goals?
4. How have the honest, confidential opinions of others affected you most?
5. Do you take time for yourself to reflect?
6. What is the best question you have ever been asked?
7. How often do you ask that best question of others?
8. Are you willing to listen to what you might not want to hear?

9. Do you realize the danger of just listening to people who agree with you?

10. How do you balance your natural tendency as a leader to act with the need to pause and reflect?

CONCLUSION

As we saw throughout these pages and the many stories within them, leading with heart is about opening yourself up to connecting with people in ways that transcend what you believed was possible. It is about creating connections with others that are honest, open, and real. Then, once those relationships are formed, it's about staying connected so those relationships can deepen. Through our connections, we can be there for each other, whether struggling through a difficult time or celebrating a milestone.

Sometimes, through those connections, we can create new possibilities. And often, when we need it most, those connections can remind us of who we are at our very best. How can we learn to lead with our hearts? It starts with knowing the sound of our hearts. Do you know what that beating sound is trying to tell you? Have you realized what your driving story is? For me, as I shared, I was driven by the fear of ever disappointing my father again. Fortunately, I was able to turn that fear, which could have been immobilizing, into a motivational force. Every leader has a driving story. I encourage you to explore the depth and meaning of yours.

Then you are poised for the next lesson, which is to open yourself up and connect with the hearts of others. This takes trust in yourself, and in the world around you. Be open and vulnerable, as you share—with honesty and compassion—your beliefs, values, hopes, and dreams with those who work shoulder to shoulder with you *and* with your customers. And look for that connection in everyone you meet.

After connecting with your own heart, and the hearts of others, you have the foundation to truly *lead with heart*. You can begin seeing the true potential of your organization—which is within the hidden talent of your employees. You can start breaking down so many barriers that your senior vice president of human resources says, "I think you're friggin' crazy." And, if you're like me, you can let yourself be comfortable with shedding a tear every now and then in front of people because they so deeply inspire you. Everything changed when I allowed myself to connect more deeply with my feelings and to share how much I truly cared about the people with whom I was working.

That is when you will see, with new lenses, that your leadership is about those you're leading more than it's about you. The "aha!" moment for me was realizing—and making the switch—from *me* to *you*. Switching from "me" to "you" made me much more effective as a leader—and much more fulfilled in my personal life. I became the leader I was meant to be when the need disappeared for me to walk into a room, thinking, "Hey, look at me!"—and I learned how to walk into a room, saying, "Hey, look at you!" While those four words may seem easy to say, when they are heartfelt the meaning makes all the difference in the world.

Ultimately, I came to realize that by being much more open and vulnerable—and connecting my heart with the hearts of others—I was breaking one of the oldest unwritten leadership rules, which, simply stated, is to keep a safe distance between yourself and those whom you are leading. Breaking that unwritten rule of leadership, for me, was cracking the code to *leading with my heart*. It opened up an entirely new way of leading for me.

I encourage you also to break that outdated rule. Break it in your own way. Break it in a way that is truly deep, personal, and meaningful for you. Get rid of the distance. Connect. Open yourself up. Believe in those with whom you decide to surround yourself. Be there for them. Help them become who they were meant to be. And give yourself the freedom to say, "Hey, look at you!"

Let me close by emphasizing that I do not mean to suggest that you can become a better leader by being more like me. Quite the contrary. My message is to be more like *you*. In fact, don't be like me and wait decades into your career before discovering how to lead with heart. Start moving in that direction now *so you can become the leader you were meant to be.*

Ask yourself some very challenging questions, because the questions we ask ourselves, and how deeply we answer them, help to shape who we become. Ask yourself:

1. Do you know what drives you?
2. Are you willing to open yourself up—to yourself and others?
3. Are you creating an engaged and trusting culture?
4. Can you be friggin' crazy?
5. When you walk in a room, do you say, "Hey, look at me!" or "Hey, look at you!"?
6. When you have difficult conversations, are they built on a foundation of honesty and trust?
7. Is your purpose compelling and your strategy clearly articulated?
8. Have you opened yourself to unvarnished advice you may not want to hear?
9. Are you willing to make the transition to business being personal—very personal?
10. Have you built your scorecard?

I encourage you not to let yourself off the hook until you know, deep in your heart, that you have answered those questions in a way that rings true to you. That is when you will genuinely know the sound of your own heart. Then surround yourself with people who encourage you to be the leader you were meant to be. And connect with them on a very deep level.

When all is said and done, the greatest gift I received was the freedom to be the leader I was meant to be. My hope for you is that you give yourself that freedom—the freedom to lead with your heart and become the leader *you* were meant to be.

MY SCORECARD UPDATE

At the end of 2014, I made the decision to retire from Avis Budget Group. This was a time of deep reflection, and of having open and honest conversations with myself—and those with whom I am close. And when my scorecard told me that on a personal level it was time for me to move on, I had to believe.

I was not sure what would happen next. But I opened myself up. I thought about how, when I received my diploma from the College of St. Thomas, and I knew I could leave the steel fabricating plant where I was working during the day, I spray-painted my work boots gold and placed them on the dining room table as a centerpiece. Sometimes you just need to open yourself up to new possibilities, to switch gears, and to believe.

FAMILY FIRST

Most significantly, on a personal level, one thing this new season allowed me to do was spend more time with my family. Right after I retired, my son Kevin and daughter-in-law, Whitney, had a son, Jackson Thomas. I was there at his birth, and I have been to every other major event with him, from baptism to birthday parties, and I have had him up at the lake all summer.

Then in August of that year, my daughter Sara and son-in-law David had a premature son, Tommy, born at twenty-seven weeks. He weighed just one pound and eleven ounces. Because my schedule was freer, my wife and I were able to be in Dallas several times to support my daughter and her husband. Then, six months to the day after he was born, little Tommy came home from the hospital. And I got to hold him for the first time. He has made extraordinary progress. There are still a lot of obstacles to overcome, but he is doing remarkably well.

Then in February of last year, my daughter Lizzie and her husband, Joe, had their first child, Vincent Thomas. He will see me at all his major events as well.

I would not have been able to do each of those things—to be there when Jack, Tommy, and Vincent were born, or to go trick-or-treating on Halloween with my granddaughter, Avery, or to spend time at the lake in the summers with my entire family, or to build a playground, or take golf lessons—if I were not able to go through the transition and begin a new stage of my life.

MORE THAN A GOLF GAME

Shortly after I retired, I received a call from John Cozzi, a partner of AEA Investors, who asked if I wanted to play a round of golf with him. AEA is a private equity firm founded by the Rockefeller, Mellon, and Harriman family interests and S. G. Warburg & Co.

Did that call come out of the blue? Not really. It was part of a much earlier connection, which I could not have possibly imagined would have led where it did. When John and I first met, I was the president of JohnsonDiversey, and his firm initially had been interested in acquiring one of our business units, then decided otherwise.

Why did John and I stay in touch? I'll let him explain: "When I was introduced to Tom, he quickly did two things. First, we were struggling to figure out what some banker had written about the organization. And Tom cleared it up in a minute. Then, after negotiating a few days, we had reached an impasse, and, for various reasons, it seemed obvious to us that this was not going to go anywhere. Then Tom came up with a perfectly reasonable solution that was a win for everyone. It was very clear to me that he has an uncanny ability to simplify—to reduce complex issues to their most essential elements. Combine that with the fact that he is an excellent judge of people—and that people like to follow him. That is a very powerful combination."

Yet, for various reasons, the deal did not consummate. Still, John said, "It was clear to me, as we were going through this, that Tom was a much different thinker and actor. So, we connected on a personal level, as well as on a strategic level."

And we stayed in touch over the years.

So, while playing golf, John asked if I would like to be a senior advisor with his organization—and I accepted in a heartbeat.

Now, as board member of two public companies, and as a senior advisor with AEA, I am coaching leaders, helping them discover what is best in themselves—and others.

What have I learned? *It all comes back to knowing who you are, then sharing of yourself, caring about others, and deepening your connections.*

A SPECIAL LIFELONG CONNECTION

After my father died, there was a man, Dr. Tom, who filled a huge void that I'd had. He has taught me a lot about what really matters, in so many ways. And he certainly taught me the importance of staying connected. My father was so fortunate to have a friend like Dr. Tom. And I was fortunate that, after my dad passed away, Dr. Tom stayed close with me my entire life. If you have a friend like that, you don't need many.

Dr. Tom was my father's best friend, and his wife, Audrey, was a dear friend to my mom. When I was growing up, he was like an uncle to me. While his patients called him Dr. Votel, I always called him Dr. Tom, and his wife I knew as Auntie Audrey.

When I was a kid, I would run with Bridgette and Tommy, the two of Dr. Tom's six children who were closest to me in age, through his spacious, grand old English Tudor, nestled on an acre on Summit Avenue, just down the street from the governor's residence, and F. Scott Fitzgerald's birth house, and just shy of four hundred other historic homes built from 1855 through the 1920s. In the summers, our families would vacation together at Gull Lake in Brainerd, Minnesota, where all the kids would sleep outside in tents between the two cabins that our parents rented along with some of their other friends and family.

One day not that long ago, I was sitting at Dr. Tom's kitchen table, eating Reuben sandwiches (his favorite) that he had just picked up from Cecil's Deli in St. Paul. As he savored a bite, I asked him to remind me, as he had many times before, how he and my father met.

"Mel and I hit it off right away," he recalled. "We used to walk home from Cretin High School together every day. For me, that was three miles. And Mel lived about halfway. It might have been because we both came from marginal neighborhoods, and most of the kids at Cretin came from families who had some means, but Mel and I just connected. We both had jobs at school to help pay for our tuitions. I remember I used to fill the coal hopper every morning."

Dr. Tom described my dad. "Mel was a tall, handsome guy, who always looked like he just stepped out of a band-box," he recalled. "He was a track star, who always exercised and was in great shape." Laughing, he said, "In fact, his nickname at Cretin was Barbell Mel. Then, as he got older, I remember, he started losing his hair, so he just shaved it all off, which was very unusual back then. That made him really stand out."

My parents stayed close with Dr. Tom and Auntie Audrey. "We had a lot of fun together," Dr. Tom said. "Your parents were great dancers. They were something to watch. And all the little moments that occurred in life seemed to bring us closer." He paused, then added, "I still have a picture of Mel on the wall going to the rec room. I see it every day when I go up and down those stairs."

When my mother called home to tell me that my dad was in the hospital in Mexico, the next call she made was to Dr. Tom. He described the call from his perspective. "I could hear Mel in the background saying, 'I feel like I'm going to die,' and she kept assuring him that everything would be okay." Dr. Tom paused, then said, "That was the last time I heard his voice. I do miss him."

When tragedy strikes, people often can be there to support each other in powerful ways. Then, while they have the best of intentions to stay in touch, it can be easy for life to somehow get in the way, and memories fade. But that was not the case with Dr. Tom and Auntie Audrey. "Mel's death further deepened our relationships," Dr. Tom said. Putting his sandwich down, he looked at me, then added, "You have always been part of our family. It has always been more than just friends between us."

Then he said to me, "This book is what you would have to write. Your entire life, you have exuded genuine affection for people, and I am sure you could not turn it off in the workplace. In fact, your message about encouraging people to connect more deeply on a personal level at work is exactly what, I believe, is now missing in the medical profession.

And it is a shame, because it used to be there. I loved practicing medicine during the golden years when there was much more compassion, caring, and concern, when doctors and patients were all people—not merely subscribers and providers."

Dr. Tom, who is now ninety-one, once had an old-fashioned family practice, where, if someone had an earache or was running a fever, he would stop by their house on his way home from his office every night. He epitomized what it means to make a personal connection.

I learned from Dr. Tom how important it is to stay connected to people, and that lifelong lesson has infused my beliefs and deepened my life. Thank you, Dr. Tom.

ACKNOWLEDGMENTS

I want to share my heartfelt thanks to the twenty-thousand-plus men and women who made up the Avis Budget Group work family of North America.

In addition, I want to extend a special *thank you* to those with whom I had the privilege of working directly, including Beth Arnold, Joe Ferraro, Gina Bruzzichesi, Ned Linnen, Jeannie Haas, Ed Sorensen, Kaye Cellie, Mike Schmidt, Yvonne Trupiano, Neil Schamus, Priscilla Alvarado, John O'Neill, Beth Kinerk, Joe Siino, Izzy Martins, David Crowther, Bob Lambert, Mike James, Paul Gallagher, and Kristen Maloney.

Then, of course, there is Pat Siniscalchi, Gerard Insall, David Blaskey, David Wyshner, and Ron Nelson.

Also, a very special thanks to all who were interviewed for this book, including Barb Gartland, Ron Nelson, Pat Siniscalchi, Andre Meesschaert, Baron Carlson, Gina Bruzzichesi, Dave Ridley, Margaret Thompson, Ned Linnen,

Bob Chaps, Barbara Kogen, Beth Kinerk, Stephen Wright, Tom Villani, Kevin Gartland, Adam Johnson, Chris McIntyre, Steve Stricker, Tim Stratman, Jack Lachenmayer, Norb Gambuzza, Chris Soder, John Cozzi, and, of course, Dr. Tom Votel.

For their steadfast belief in this project since its inception, their ongoing encouragement, and their insightful suggestions, we thank our consummate agent Lorin Rees, our exceptionally talented editors Leah Wilson and Debbie Harmsen, and our impeccable copyeditor James Fraleigh.

And for his inspiration and continued support of this project, thank you to Captain D. Michael Abrashoff, former commander of the USS *Benfold*, and *New York Times* and *Wall Street Journal* business bestselling author of *It's Your Ship*.

Finally, my sincere thanks to Tim Finchem, former commissioner of the PGA Tour, for writing such a beautiful, inspiring, and heartfelt foreword.

ABOUT THE AUTHORS

 TOM GARTLAND is a compassionate, strategic, and inspiring author, speaker, and leader who helped transform the culture of a Fortune 500 company into an engaged, collaborative, top-performing organization that experienced unprecedented growth.

Currently a member of the board of directors of two publicly traded companies (Xenia Hotels and ABM), and a senior advisor to a private equity firm founded by the Rockefeller, Mellon, and Harriman family interests and S. G. Warburg & Co. (AEA Investors), Tom is the former president, North America, for Avis Budget Group (2011–2014).

Tom was responsible at Avis Budget Group for the daily management of more than 20,000 employees in

5,000 locations, overseeing over 350,000 vehicles, which accounted for more than $5 billion in annual revenue.

He received a bachelor's degree in business administration/marketing from the University of St. Thomas, where he is on the Board of Governors at Opus College.

As Tom has said, "My leadership philosophy can be summed up in nine words: *When we focus on people, the profits will follow*." To find out more about Tom's book and speeches, visit his website: www.LeadWithHeart.com.

PATRICK SWEENEY is an inspiring executive coach and leadership consultant, who has written and coauthored four books, including the *New York Times* bestseller *Succeed on Your Own Terms*. He connects, challenges, and collaborates with executives, transforming their thought leadership into compelling books and speeches that position them and their organizations for success. Patrick is also an engaging keynote speaker who has presented around the world, including the China Economic Forum and HSM in Brazil. The former president of an international consulting firm, and speechwriter for a governor, Patrick holds a master's degree in positive psychology from the University of Pennsylvania.

To find out more about this book or inquire about Tom's availability to present a keynote speech, visit his website: www.LeadWithHeart.com.